FACILITATOR'S GUIDE

HIRING THE BEST PERSON
FOR EVERY JOB
FOR EVERY JOB

FACILITATOR'S GUIDE

HIRING THE BEST PERSON
FOR EVERY JOB

DeANNE ROSENBERG

JOSSEY-BASS/PFEIFFER
A Wiley Company
www.pfeiffer.com

Published by

JOSSEY-BASS/PFEIFFER

A Wiley Company
989 Market Street
San Francisco, CA 94103-1741
415.433.1740; Fax 415.433.0499
800.274.4434; Fax 800.569.0443

www.pfeiffer.com

Jossey-Bass/Pfeiffer is a registered trademark of John Wiley & Sons, Inc.

ISBN: 0-7879-5896-4

Printed in the United States of America

We at Jossey-Bass strive to use the most environmentally sensitive paper stocks available to us. Our publications are printed on acid-free recycled stock whenever possible, and our paper always meets or exceeds minimum GPO and EPA requirements.

Acquiring Editor: Josh Blatter
Director of Development: Kathleen Dolan Davies
Developmental Editor: Susan Rachmeler
Editor: Rebecca Taff
Senior Production Editor: Dawn Kilgore
Manufacturing Supervisor: Becky Carreño
Cover Design: Bruce Lundquist and Chris Wallace
Illustrations: Lotus Art

Printing 10   9   8   7   6   5   4   3   2   1

CONTENTS

INTRODUCTION

THE PURPOSE OF THIS TRAINING PACKAGE is to assist you in presenting a "no-fail" interviewing strategy to managers and to others who interview candidates in order to add personnel to their staff.

If your participants are like most managers, "interviewing" is not a priority area of concern for them. It is done intuitively, on the spur of the moment, and without much preparation. Since they may only interview a few times a year, they remain novices at the process.

Studies from the U.S. Department of Labor indicate that 50 percent of all new hires leave the job within the first six months.* It is the mission of this training package to rectify these dreadful statistics—at least for your participants—by offering them a logical, intelligent, repeatable strategy that is easy to apply.

The personal interview can and should be an accurate predictor of future job performance if preceded by a precise analysis of the position and thoughtful preparation prior to the interview. The process advanced in this training package will take your participants step-by-step through five basic areas:

1. Analyzing the core responsibilities of the position;

2. Clearly determining the manager's performance expectations regarding those core responsibilities;

3. Determining what skills, knowledge, experience, attributes, and competencies are needed to meet those performance expectations and responsibilities;

Source: The categories and percentages are based on a 1990 study done by The Society for Human Resource Management and published in the December 1990 issue of *Personnel Journal*; financial data is based on 2000 salary figures.

4. Generating appropriate questions that, when answered, will provide solid evidence of the candidate's possession or lack of those required qualities; and

5. Designing and utilizing a structured format (the Master Match Matrix®) to support an evaluation process of the interviewing data.

The process you are about to present to your participants is somewhat unique:

- The analysis of the job's requirements is based on the manager's performance expectations;

- The basis for the evaluation of the candidate's viability is done prior to speaking with a single candidate; and

- Scant use is made of the candidate's resume.

The training package offers your participants:

- A logical, intelligent, repeatable strategy that is easy to apply;

- A strategy that recognizes managers want to spend a minimum amount of time on the interview;

- A method that will generate superior results *every* time it is used; and

- A system that demonstrates that a person needs only ten good questions and 40 minutes to do an excellent job of interviewing.

Components of the Training Package

This training package consists of two parts: the Facilitator's Guide, which contains a CD-ROM, and the Participant Workbook. The CD-ROM is also available for purchase separately for participant use. Also available separately is a book, *A Manager's Guide to Hiring the Best Person for Every Job* (Rosenberg, 2000), which is necessary for anyone leading the training workshop.

The Facilitator's Guide contains the following:

- Step-by-step instructions for leading a one- or two-day workshop;

- A set of character role-play cards to be used in a role-play activity;

- A set of transparency masters; and

- A CD-ROM that includes templates and an expanded list of interview questions organized by desired competency.

The Participant Workbook contains relevant information, forms, exercises, and resources for the participants to use during and after the workshop.

Workshop Learning Objectives

By the end of this workshop, your participants will be able to

- Design a strategy for a more targeted approach to the interview based on the Master Match Matrix®;

- Make a decision about a candidate's strengths and weaknesses within 40 minutes;

- Develop effective question-generation techniques based on specific job objectives;

- Utilize a variety of questioning techniques to be used in interviews;

- Match candidate and questioning technique for maximum data collection;

- Separate listening from evaluation during the interview process;

- Use active listening techniques;

- Understand and "read" the hidden meanings in body language;

- Recognize the Equal Opportunity restrictions and discuss their implications for the interview process; and

- Utilize two theoretical approaches to interviewing, Interviewing by Objectives and McClelland's Theory of Personality Fit (known as *People Reading*).

In addition, each participant will leave the workshop with his or her own, individually developed Master Match Matrix® to use when interviewing staff for that particular position.

In the Words of a Master Trainer . . .

- Teaching methods must be interactive and experiential because the more a person contributes to his or her own learning, the more effective that learning will be.

- Participants will learn as much from themselves and from one another as they will from you. Your job, therefore, is to give them information and to make the space safe so that the other two-thirds of the learning can happen.

- People's interest is captured by illustrative stories and vignettes, not by theory and explanation. Stories help them to see what you are saying in their minds' eye. Season your presentation with stories that illustrate your points.

- People will not always learn exactly what you intended for them to learn, but that must be alright with you.

- Trust the process; don't try to "manage" or control it.

- Questions need to be answered when asked. Even though such interruptions may be annoying to you and disruptive to the presentation flow, it is important to the learning process that—whenever feasible—questions be answered when asked.

- There are two secrets about teaching adults: adults learn best by doing and adults learn best when there is an apparent related flow between topics.

- To that end, each topic is laid out in such a way as to flow seamlessly from one into the next. In other words, do NOT change the arrangement of topics from how they are presented in the Facilitator's Guide and/or the Participant Workbook.

- When addressing the participants, always include yourself as a learner. That is, use "we" rather than "you." *Example:* "When *we* interview, *we* sometimes fall into the bad habit of only listening to the candidate with half *our* attention. The other half is on *our* workload and all the tasks that have been put on hold while *we* talk to this person who probably will not be right for *our* needs anyway."

- In any random group of twenty participants, 55 percent will probably be visual learners; 35 percent will probably be kinesthetic learners; and 10 percent will probably be auditory learners (O'Connor & Seymour, 1994).

- This workshop format has been designed to capture the interest and attention of all three types of learners. You will be providing the auditory learning material through lecture. The Participant Workbook has been designed to accommodate note taking for the visual and kinesthetic learners. Therefore, encourage note taking as you move through the course material. Observing the video and seeing what you place on the overhead projector and flip charts (use color whenever possible) will assist the visual learners to master the material, and role playing will assist the kinesthetic learners to master the material. (These participants need to experience in order to absorb the material.)

- You will notice that the recommended room arrangements (pages xvii and xix) include two flip charts with easels, one on each side of the facilitator's presentation table. This training design is designed

(a) to help you in presenting the material to a variety of learners and (b) to assist you in maintaining control of the direction and flow of the group discussions.

- You will find it helpful to the learning process of the visual learners if you illustrate your remarks with stick figures, flow charts, or characters of some kind. (Always use colored markers.) Put those on one flip chart and use the other flip chart to record words and phrases. Make use of the flip charts as often as possible throughout the workshop.

- Invariably, a participant will interrupt with a perfectly reasonable question that you intend to answer two hours from now when you are covering that topic. The problem is how to deal with that participant's question without derailing the flow of your presentation now and without insulting the participant. You will find the use of the second flip chart—the one for words and phrases—remarkably handy here. Just go over to the flip chart, ask the participant to repeat his or her question, and write the question on the flip chart. Try to capture it word-for-word; then say, "We will be covering that issue in just a little while, but I am writing it here to ensure that we do discuss it." Participants tend to repeat themselves until they are certain they have been heard. Writing the question for all to see ensures that the participant will not interrupt you again with that same question.

- Remember that you are the most important visual aid in the entire learning process. If you are excited about what you are teaching, the participants will be excited about what they are learning. Stay active and move.

Workshop Formats

This Facilitator's Guide includes two workshop formats: a one-day format and a two-day format. Both formats cover similar ground. The two-day format, however, offers more in-depth information and many more specific fine points of interviewing. These additional segments have been identified as material that should be skipped if you are conducting the one-day workshop.

The most effective workshop in terms of skill retention and depth of learning is the two-day (consecutive) format. If at all possible, try to influence your organization to support you in presenting the two-day (consecutive) program.

On the following pages, you will find the suggested schedule for both the one- and two-day workshops.

Workshop Schedule (One-Day Format)

8:30	Introduction, Interviewing Quiz, Cost of a Poor Hire	30 min
9:00	Interviewing by Objectives, Master Match Matrix®, Strategy	1 hr 30 min
10:30	Break	15 min
10:45	Techniques for Interviewing, Question Generation, Listening Visually (Body Language Cues)	1 hr
11:45	Lunch	45 min
12:30	Preparation for Role-Play Activity	30 min
1:00	Live Role Play	1 hr
2:00	Break	15 min
2:15	Legal Restrictions and Related Issues: Questions One Can and Cannot Ask During an Interview, Checking and Giving References and Employer Liability	45 min
3:00	People Reading: Interviewing for Personality Fit	1 hr
4:00	Wrap-Up	30 min
4:30	Adjournment	

Workshop Schedule (Two-Day Format)

Day One

8:30	Introduction, Interviewing Quiz, Cost of a Poor Hire	30 min
9:00	Interviewing by Objectives, Master Match Matrix®, Strategy	1 hr 30 min
10:30	Break	15 min
10:45	Pre-Planning the Interview	45 min
11:30	Lunch	45 min
12:15	Techniques for Interviewing, Question Generation, Listening Visually (Body Language Cues)	1 hr
1:15	Advanced Questioning Challenges: Getting the Shy Candidate to Speak, Making Questions More Productive, Making the Interview More Conversational, Dumb Questions, Responding to Evasion Tactics	45 min
2:00	Break	15 min

2:15	Advanced Interviewing Strategies: Resume Analysis, Record Keeping and Related Paperwork, Rapid Screening Techniques, Round Robin and Team Interviews, Interviewing by Telephone, Hiring Professionals	45 min
3:00	*Previously Taped Interviews (video), Discussion and Critique	1 hr
4:00	Participant Preparation for Role-Play Activity (Homework)	15 min
4:15	Wrap-Up	15 min
4:30	Adjournment	

Workshop Schedule (Two-Day Format)
Day Two

8:30	Legal Restrictions and Related Issues: Questions One Can and Cannot Ask During an Interview, Checking and Giving References and Employer Liability	45 min
9:15	Break	15 min
9:30	Live Role Play	2 hr 45 min
12:15	Lunch	45 min
1:00	Video Playback, Discussion and Critique	2 hr
3:00	Break	15 min
3:15	People Reading: Interviewing for Personality Fit	1 hr
4:15	Wrap-Up	30 min
4:45	Adjournment	

Audiovisual Equipment Required
One-Day Format

- Overhead projector

- Screen

- Two flip charts with easels

Two-Day Format

- Overhead projector

- Screen

- Two flip charts with easels

*After your first session, you will have your own videotapes of actual interviews to show to succeeding classes.

- Video camera, monitor, playback unit
- Two microphones for the role players
- One small breakout room (for videotaping)
- Blank videotape

Room Logistics

Seating arrangements for both workshop formats *must* encourage audience participation. The "Dinner Style" (using rectangular tables) or the "Buzz Style" (using round tables) accomplishes this. Participants should be seated so that there are five people to each table and no one has his or her back toward you.

Interviewing is a skill. The only way people can learn a skill is to do it—practice it and have coaching and feedback immediately available. However, it is critical that participants not be embarrassed as they attempt to master the skill. To minimize potential embarrassment, seat participants in groups of five where two people role play at a time (with one person playing the candidate and the other playing the manager who is seeking an addition to his or her staff) while the other three members of the group listen, take notes, and observe. Then, when the role play is finished, those observing provide feedback to the person playing the manager. In this way, no one performs in front of the entire group.

The issue of embarrassment during a role play is not an issue for participants in the two-day workshop format because participants have had so much interaction already by the end of the first day that they feel quite comfortable with one another.

Set a 4-foot by 5-foot table in the front of the room on which the overhead projector can be placed, along with the appropriate transparencies. You will find it helpful to auditory, visual, and kinesthetic learners if you lecture from that position and illustrate your points on the overhead projector as you speak. This will give your lecture material a fresh, rather than a canned feeling. Place the two flip-chart easels so that there is one on each side of the overhead projector table. The video playback unit (for the two-day format) should be placed at the back of the room, well out of the way, as illustrated in the diagrams.

1st DAY - ONE-DAY FORMAT

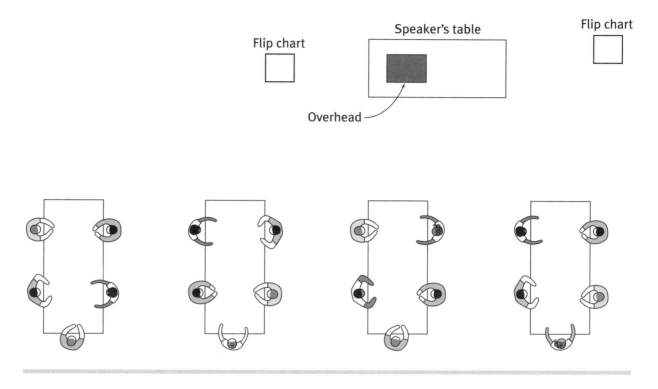

Flip chart

Speaker's table

Flip chart

Overhead

1st DAY - TWO-DAY FORMAT

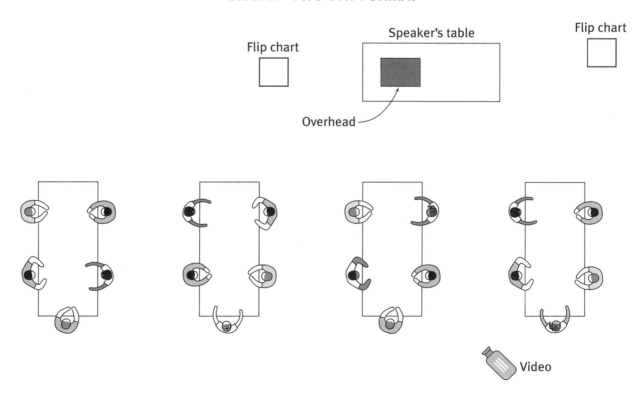

Flip chart

Speaker's table

Flip chart

Overhead

Video

For the second day of the two-day format, push all the tables together so that all the participants are seated facing one another in a large group (conference style). In this way, everyone will be able to hear and provide feedback to the live interviews that will take place while pairs are interviewing before the video in private in the adjacent breakout room. The diagrams on the next page illustrate the suggested layout.

Using the Facilitator's Guide

This Facilitator's Guide has been designed to assist you in presenting the best learning experience possible. It will take you through each segment step-by-step, enabling you to teach the various pieces in the most effective learning sequence possible. In each segment, you will find references to the appropriate pages in the Participant Workbook as well as to pages in *A Manager's Guide to Hiring the Best Person for Every Job,* where you can find additional material to augment your training.

The program contains a tremendous amount of material, so suggested time frames for each activity are included to help ensure that you can cover all topics and activities. Be aware, however, that unless you keep things moving along at a vigorous pace, you will not be able to cover everything.

Preparation

It is strongly recommended that you not attempt to teach this workshop without first reading *A Manager's Guide to Hiring the Best Person for Every Job.* This will give you the knowledge and expertise to answer the participants' questions. It will also provide you with the self-confidence to present this innovative and somewhat controversial strategy for interviewing.

You should also read through the entire Facilitator's Guide and Participant Workbook prior to conducting the training and become familiar with the content of both pieces. At the end of the Facilitator's Guide are thirteen "role cards." Prior to presenting the workshop, duplicate these onto different colored index stock or construction paper for the role-play portion of the workshop. Using colored paper allows you to more easily identify each "character." The color and texture of the paper will also appeal to your visual and kinesthetic learners. For the one-day workshop, each participant will need *one* of the role cards. For the two-day workshop, each participant will need *two* different cards at the appropriate times.

2nd DAY - TWO-DAY FORMAT

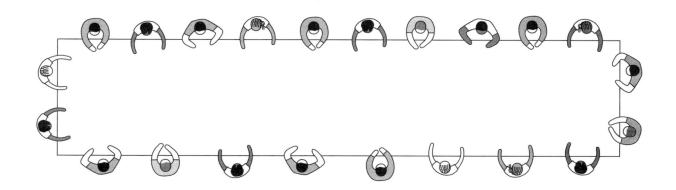

 Video

VIDEO BREAKOUT ROOM - TWO-DAY FORMAT, 2nd DAY

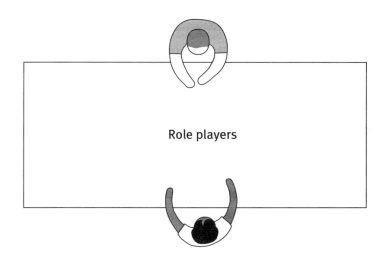

Role players

Video operator and camera

 Video

When you send out the announcement of the workshop, make certain that each participant understands that he or she is to come to the workshop with a copy of *his or her own resume.* Old, out-of-date ones will work just fine. If participants tell you that they do not have resumes, ask them to construct a very *brief* one covering just their present job and educational background.

At the very beginning of the workshop, you will be covering the topic of the cost of turnover. Some specific dollar costs have been provided. However, to make the topic more real for your participants, you might ask human resources for some actual cost figures your organization has been forced to bear due to poor hiring practices. If you are able to obtain actual figures, prepare additional copies to distribute to the participants. This would be a great tool to create the pressure for learning.

The day of the workshop, make sure you come prepared with your Facilitator's Guide, any necessary transparencies, and enough Participant Workbooks so that each participant will have one at the start of the workshop. Provide pens or pencils also, if necessary.

Using the Participant Workbook

As you teach this course, keep a copy of the Participant Workbook handy so that you can direct the attendees to the appropriate pages. The Participant Workbook contains:

1. Outlines of the lecture material with space for the attendees to take notes. Taking notes helps the learning process for both visual and kinesthetic learners, so be sure to encourage note taking.

2. Exercises with *suggested time frames* to assure the learning of each topic presented. You will find it helpful if you introduce the concept of the exercises to the participants by saying something like the following:

    "The exercises in your workbook, which we will be completing after each segment, are an opportunity to test yourself. The most effective way to go through these exercises is to do them as rapidly as possible. They are designed to find out where you might need more information. And of course, no one but you will ever see your scores."

The activities can be done as a group exercise (less effective in terms of the learning value) where you read the problem aloud to the participants and ask for responses from the group as a whole. Then discuss the answers provided with the group.

You can also instruct the participants to fill out and then score the exercises on their own. (This is a more effective learning strategy, especially for the visual and kinesthetic learners.) Then, after everyone has completed and scored the exercise, ask the participants whether anyone has any questions or wishes further clarification.

Answers to all the exercises are located at the back of the Participant Workbook.

3. Forms and templates to assist participants in clarifying their thinking and decision-making processes during all phases of the interviewing and selection activity.

4. Strategy information that participants can use as referral material long after the workshop is completed. During the workshop, you want to refer the participants to these items for a quick glance, just to ensure that they know those items are there and available to them (*example:* "Completing the MMM®," "Common Errors in Conducting the Interview," etc.).

5. An appendix of interview questions listed by competency desired. (The CD-ROM is also available for purchase separately for participant use.)

6. A list of resources for further information on various topics.

INTRODUCING THE WORKSHOP

Time	Materials
One-Day	Transparency 1
8:30—9:00 am (30 min)	Participant Workbook,
Two-Day	pages ix–xiii
8:30—9:00 am (1st day)	Overhead projector
(30 min)	

IT IS PROBABLY SAFE TO ASSUME that many of the participants attending your workshop do not want to be there. They may feel they have more important work awaiting their attention and, moreover, they already know how to interview. You need to establish a desire to learn what you are about to offer. You have two tools available for you to create that desire:

1. The Interviewing Quiz (see pages xi–xii in the Participant Workbook), which tests the participants' basic knowledge of interviewing, and

2. The explanation of the cost of turnover (see page xiii in the Participant Workbook and Transparency 1).

 As the participants arrive and receive their workbooks, place Transparency 1 on the projector and say the following:

> "While we are waiting for the rest of the participants to arrive, please read over pages ix and x in the workbook so that you understand why we are here. Then take the Interview Quiz on pages xi and xii. See just how good your knowledge of the topic is. The answers to the quiz can be found on pages A-7 through A-9 at the back of your workbook."

Please note that you will NOT be discussing the results of the Interviewing Quiz nor the information shown on page xiii of the Participant

Workbook and on Transparency 1. These two items serve two very important purposes:

1. To create the desire to learn:
   - "Gee wiz, I guess I didn't know as much about interviewing as I though I did."
   - "Wow! Interviewing mistakes really are costly."
2. To keep the early arrivals occupied while the latecomers are arriving.

Please also *allow people to sit wherever they want.* In the first place, participants already know the workshop will involve role playing. Many people become anxious about role playing, which reduces their ability to learn. You want them—at least initially—to feel as comfortable as possible. Secondly, people generally sit with their immediate co-workers. This fact may be of great help to you when the time comes to pair up participants (with similar hiring needs) for the role-play activity.

Begin your presentation by referring participants to the Workshop Objectives presented on page ix of the Participant Workbook. Then go over the day's agenda so people know when breaks and lunch are scheduled. Once that is completed, go around the room and ask each participant the following questions:

1. "How long have you been interviewing?"
2. "What particular issues do you want to be covered in this workshop?"
3. "What are the positions (job titles) for which you most often seek candidates?"

Take notes on their responses and keep those handy to ensure that you cover those issues. In addition, the information gained from question 3 will assist you in pairing people up for the role-play activities later on in the workshop.

INTERVIEWING BY OBJECTIVES AND USING THE MASTER MATCH MATRIX®

Time	Materials
One-Day	Transparencies 1–5
9:00—10:30 am (1 hr 30 min)	Participant Workbook, pages 1–18
Two-Day	
9:00—10:30 am (1st day)	Book, pages 32–86
(1 hr 30 min)	Overhead projector
	Colored markers
	Two flip charts with easels
	Blank transparencies

Victimization of the Untrained Interviewer

Begin your presentation by discussing Victimization of the Untrained Interviewer (see pages 32–36 of the book). Here is a good opening speech.

"Employment selection is a risky business because you are buying something before you know how well it will work. I wonder how many of you would purchase an expensive piece of equipment—say an automobile—without first researching such things as gas mileage, repair costs, safety record, and resale value. If you had a friend who had owned a similar car, you might even ask what his or her experience had been with the vehicle (references). And yet we make the decision to hire based on 20 to 30 minutes of conversation during which we do most of the talking. Now how are you going to learn anything if you are doing all the talking?

"So we minimize the exchange of facts and we often rely on education, previous job longevity, and verbal agility during the interview to make the hiring decision for us."

Place Transparency 1 on the projector again to illustrate the fallacy of making hiring decisions on that basis. If you were able to obtain some actual cost figures your organization has been forced to bear due to poor hiring practices, now would be the time to distribute them. It will make the topic more real for your participants.

Direct participants to page 1 of the Participant Workbook and encourage them to take notes. In your presentation, be sure to cover the following points.

Untrained interviewers often allow themselves to be victimized by the apparent relevance of experience, education, and verbal agility:

- *Apparent Relevance of Experience.* "Job hopping" is not always a negative; these folks have often gained valuable knowledge and skills in a variety of areas. Long tenure does not always ensure greater learning.

- *Apparent Relevance of Education.* GPA is not correlated to job success. An Ivy League education will not necessarily ensure success, although it generally costs more to hire these people.

- *Apparent Relevance of Verbal Agility.* The point of the interview is not to have a friendly conversation; the goal should be to ascertain whether or not the candidate meets the job requirements. Facility with conversation is no guarantee of success, although many interviewers may be inclined to recommend people because they "liked" them or were impressed by them.

The Four Criteria Traditionally Used for Selection

Segue into explaining how interviewing has been done traditionally (see pages 38–50 of the book). Place Transparency 2 on the projector. The points to be covered in this segment follow:

1. Personal Preferences of the Interviewer

An untrained interviewer tends to hire people like him- or herself, someone who thinks like the interviewer, perhaps sees the world as the interviewer does, maybe hails from the same part of the country.

- *The Halo Effect.* The interviewer finds that he or she and the candidate have something in common, and this positively affects the interview. Even if something negative is uncovered, the interviewer is likely to brush it aside.

- *Use of Gut-Level Messages.* Sometimes, despite a candidate's seeming well-qualified, the interviewer will feel that the person is not right for the job. Despite the interviewer's inability to name the problem, these gut-level feelings are frequently accurate. They are usually the result of subtle clues that the interviewer picks up from the candidate, along with his or her knowledge of the job.

2. Personality Traits of the Candidate

Prior to 1971, employers used all kinds of tests to assess traits like intelligence, initiative, drive, and loyalty. In 1971, the federal courts struck down such testing as discriminatory and said that any test to be used as a pre-employment evaluation had to be validated. Since then, tests for some specific fields (accounting, engineering, sales) have been developed and are commercially available. In addition, some organizations developed their own validated tests by assessing employees after they had been hired and working for at least six months. By and large, however, few organizations utilize such tests today.

3. Educational Background of the Candidate

At one time, many organizations tried to fill all jobs with college graduates. They frequently ended up with bored, overqualified employees. Organizations also frequently believed that an Ivy League graduate would be more successful than, say, a state university graduate. Despite this tendency, educational background may or may not be germane to a specific job.

Interviewers need to look at other factors, too, such as elective courses, extracurricular activities, and employment while in school.

4. Behavioral Skills of the Candidate

Candidates bring two classes of skills with them, mental and physical. Behavioral skills are the name given to the physical skills.

Physical Tests

Don't just ask about a skill; have the candidate perform, for example, take a typing test or a dexterity test or actually make change. This works for jobs that require obvious physical skills.

Verbal Tests

For people whose skills—such as analytical thinking, team leadership, or creativity—are more difficult to ascertain, the interviewer may be able to test these skills by asking a set of ten well-thought-out questions. Fewer than ten questions may not be enough to scan the depth and breadth of the candidate's skill and experience. All questions should meet two criteria:

- They must be framed so that candidates cannot discern a *right* answer (the answer they think you want to hear).

- The interviewer must know the response he or she is seeking *before* asking the question.

Three of the best types of such investigative questions are formatted as follows:

- *What if...?* These questions give candidates an opportunity to respond to real life situations that already exist in an organization (so the interviewer already knows what the best avenue is for their resolution and why).

- *What has been your experience with...?* These questions give candidates an opportunity to talk about specific examples from their personal experiences.

- *What has been the most challenging...?* These questions give candidates an opportunity to talk about their problem-solving skills and their creativity.

Differences Between Behavioral and Puzzle Questions

This is the point at which you want to ensure that the participants understand the difference between "behavioral" questions and "puzzle" questions (see pages 50–54 in the book). Understanding the difference between these two types of questions is *critical* to the development of effective interviewing strategy. Introduce this topic by saying:

"There is a tremendous difference between questions that begin with the words *what if* ... and questions that ask *what has been your experience with* ...? Can anyone tell me what that difference is?"

After participants have offered their explanations, say the following:

"Puzzle questions ask what the candidates *would do* in a situation (future oriented). Behavioral questions ask what the candidate *actually did* in past situations.

"Behavioral questions ask how candidates use what they know or how they react (in spite of what they know) in specific, real-life situations. Puzzle questions are used to discover how the candidate thinks. Embedded in the puzzle question is the assumption that, if the candidate has read enough books on management, he or she can probably come up with a suitable response.

"Behavioral questions target the belief that past performance is the best predictor of future performance. Such questions assume that candidates will be faced with situations in the future that will be quite similar to those faced in the past and that the resolution strategies that were used in the past will also be available in the future. This may not be so. Future situations may be quite different; if future situations are similar, the resolution strategies available will be different.

"Therefore, knowing what the candidate did in the past is not sufficient. You also want to know how candidates process information and use their reasoning ability and judgment concerning situations they may not have experienced.

"Most hiring mistakes are made because the interviewer used too many puzzle questions and not enough behavioral questions. A good interviewing strategy is made up of 75 percent behavioral questions and 25 percent puzzle questions."

Spend several minutes with the participants on turning puzzle questions into behavioral questions and vice versa. Participants must be able to hear the difference and recognize the contrast between the two. Once the group understands the difference between the two types of questions, secure the learning by asking the participants to test themselves by completing and scoring pages 3–4 (Exercise 1) in the Participant Workbook (*Suggested Time:* 5 minutes).

The Fifth Criterion: Selection by Objectives

(See pages 54–61 in the book.) Begin this section by saying the following:

"We've just reviewed the four traditional selection criteria: (1) interviewer preference, (2) personality traits of the candidate, (3) educational background of the candidate, and (4) behavioral skills of the candidate. Then we examined the difference between behavioral questions and puzzle questions. We'll now examine a new, additional criterion: selection by objectives."

Selection by objectives is the basis for the Master Match Matrix®, which will be covered in this section. It is important to cover the following points:

Recognizing Behavioral Patterns

Selection by objectives is based on the premise that past behavior patterns are likely to be repeated and that those who've succeeded in the past are likely to succeed again. Those who've had problems, for example, blaming others for their mistakes, difficulty getting along with others, manipulating the rules, exploiting others, and so forth, are likely to have those problems again, even in a different environment.

Using a Statement of Job Objectives Instead of a Job Description

A job description lists tasks and activities; job objectives list desired results and outputs. Performance expectations can become the basis for the job description (place Transparency 3 on the projector as you discuss this point).

A good way to introduce the concept of the job objectives is to say:

"If I were your candidate and I asked what would make the difference for me between being successful or being totally ineffective at this job, you would probably tell me that all I have to do is meet your performance expectations. So that is how we begin the analysis of what skill sets, background, knowledge, experience, and so forth you need in the person who will be hired into this job."

Place Transparency 4 on the projector and refer the participants to page 6 in their workbooks. Lead participants through the use of the Performance Expectations Worksheet (pages 57–61 in the book).

Help them to understand that its only function is to aid them to gain meticulous clarity on what the candidate needs to have (competencies) in order for him or her to be successful in the position. When completing the worksheet, participants should focus on the question: "What expectations, when fulfilled, will I regard as satisfactory performance?"

Work through each of the sections of the Performance Expectations Worksheet with participants, using your own example or the one on the next page to help explain each section.

Example

The job is telephone salesperson

- Focus on the five most important responsibilities, for example: "the number one responsibility would be responding to customers calling in to order our products as quickly and cordially as possible"

- List performance level in a quantifiable way whenever possible, for example: "answering the phone by the second ring; shipping orders within 24 hours"

- Determine concrete ways to measure performance, for example: "installing a device that tracks how quickly calls are picked up; comparing order dates with shipping dates"

- Based on the expectations for this responsibility, list the competencies that a successful candidate will require, for example: "good command of the English language; strong knowledge of our product line; pleasant telephone voice and manner; customer service mentality"

In order to impress on the participants that they must sort out their performance expectations *before* they can make a relevant and useful list of competencies to search for in their candidates, ask participants to turn to page 7 in their workbooks, where they will find the Competencies Required Worksheet, and say the following:

"Pretend that your organization has given you permission to hire an assistant. What competencies would you want that assistant to have? Write those competencies on the Competencies Required Worksheet."

Give participants 5 minutes to complete this activity and then ask them:

"How did you come up with those competencies? On what did you base your need for those particular competencies?"

You hope the participants will say that their selection of competencies was based on their expectations of their assistant's performance.

This is an excellent time to remind the participants that developing a list of competencies against which to judge the viability of any candidate is something *they* must do—not human resources. This is because no one knows their expectations and the actual needs of their department better than they do.

Designing and Using the Master Match Matrix®

(See book pages 62–79.) Introduce this section by saying the following:

> "There is a fairy tale that out there somewhere is the perfect candidate. Forget it! The perfect candidate does not exist. What you find is some candidates who are strong in some areas and weak in others. Therefore, you need a tool that will enable you to see clearly what your tradeoffs are. The Master Match Matrix® (MMM®) will not only clarify those tradeoffs, but will provide an objective foundation from which to launch your selection process."

To introduce the participants to the Master Match Matrix®:

- Place Transparency 5 on the projector.
- Write on it as you explain how to set up the MMM®.
- Refer participants to pages 8–9 in their workbooks.

When talking about the Master Match Matrix®, cover the following points:

- Each MMM® is position-specific;
- Once it's done, you'll rarely have to do it again;
- The competencies will probably remain the same; but
- The order of their importance may change.

Example: Let's say that today you are hiring a technical equipment buyer. The company is facing its busiest year ever. You need that new person to be very experienced. There is absolutely no time available to train. Therefore, the issue of "experience—five years as a technical equipment buyer" may be number two on your MMM®. Six months from now, things are slower because it is summer. There's lots of time available to train a new buyer, so "experience—five years as a technical equipment buyer" may fall to number six on your MMM®.

Point out that there are three steps to completing an MMM®:

1. Identify the competencies desired in broad brush strokes;
2. Clarify your meaning of the terms as specifically as possible; and
3. Work on generating questions specific to your clarified competencies.

Step 1

List the competencies in priority order and assign scores according to their importance. The example on Transparency 5 has room for eight competencies, but you could have more, in fact as many as you wish.

Scores are assigned in descending order. For example, if you have eight competencies, the first priority competency has a maximum score of 8, the second priority competency has a maximum score of 7, and so on, all the way down to the eighth priority competency, which has a maximum score of 1. If a given candidate fulfills the first priority competency requirements completely, the candidate would receive a score of 8. If not, he or she would receive a lesser score. The candidate or candidates having the highest score would either be hired or be called back for additional interviews. Show Transparency 6 as a scoring example and direct participants to page 10 in the Participant Workbook.

Step 2

The items listed on the MMM® are fairly broad. To interview successfully, you need to think in a very specific way. For example, if one of your competencies is "good communicator," do you mean verbally or in writing? Does this candidate need to communicate with various levels in the organization or with customers, suppliers, and vendors? Does this candidate need to be able to communicate with people from different cultures or for whom English is not their primary language? Does this candidate need to communicate face-to-face, on the telephone, through written reports, or by e-mail?

Step 3

Create twenty-five to thirty specific questions based on your refined expectations, of which you can reasonably expect to use ten during a 40-minute interview.

Participants will want to know why they have to prepare twenty-five or thirty thoughtful, specific questions when they only expect to utilize ten of them. You can respond to that query with the following:

"Since the design and selection of the questions comes prior to encountering a single resume or candidate, you will find it worthwhile to have a variety of appropriate questions available from which to choose those final ten.

"First of all, the candidate's paperwork might supply some of the answers to your pre-selected questions. Second, your initial conversation with the candidate might also satisfy some of your pre-selected questions. Third, the candidate's experience or lack thereof in a particular area might make asking some of those pre-selected questions irrelevant. Obviously, you are going to need more questions 'at the ready' than you will actually use.

"In addition, it might happen that, in answering one of your questions, the candidate might well provide enough data to score a number of items on the MMM®. For example, the position might require taking initiative, creativity, and analytical skills. You ask the question, 'Tell me about the most innovative approach you have ever taken to solving a problem.' The candidate responds with data on all three issues.

"Therefore, from a practical point of view, you should have twenty-five to thirty pre-selected questions ready—at least three for each of the attribute categories on the MMM®."

The most effective way to cover the issue of the three steps mentioned above is to *engage the entire group in designing an MMM® with you.* Place Transparency 7 on the projector and say:

"Let's suppose I am your human resources person and you are hiring an assistant for yourself. What competencies or abilities or experience or attributes would you want that person to have? Refer to what you have already written down on page 7 of your workbook, the Competencies Required Worksheet."

Then select a volunteer from each group to supply one attribute, skill, experience, competency, skill set, or whatever requirement he or she deems necessary for an effective assistant to possess. Start filling in those qualities *as they are given to you* right on the transparency, with the first one going into the first priority competency box. The issue of the priorities of the various competencies will be considered later on. When all eight competency boxes have been filled in, tell the group:

"You can put anything you wish on your MMM®, as long as you have a way of scoring it that satisfies you. Of course, the more definitive you make your attributes, the better the MMM® will work for you. For example, 'three years' experience as a supervisor of software developers' is better than 'supervisory experience.'

"Now some attributes are easy to score, such as number of years of experience or a degree of some kind. Others—such as 'good human relations skills' and 'team player'—are more difficult. We are going to concentrate on the more challenging ones because those are where you will gain your greatest insight regarding the candidate's viability for the position. Which of these characteristics would you like to work on as a group exercise?"

Allow the participants to select, by show of hands, which two or three attributes they wish to work on. Write those on the flip chart—one per page—and say:

"That's the first step in setting up the MMM®. The second step is to gain as much clarity as possible for yourself on exactly what you mean by these expansive terms, because these are really not precise enough to be useful. The fact is that each one of us has a little bit different idea on exactly what these broadly based terms actually mean. So let's say that, as your human resource person, I come back to you with this MMM® you have so nicely filled out and I tell you [address yourself to the participant who provided you with the first competency selected], 'I'm not really clear on exactly what you mean when you say you need someone who is a "self-starter." Can you give me a little more detail on that requirement?' And you would answer by telling me, 'I need someone who . . .'"

Let the participant explain that requirement in more detail while you capture the essence of his or her explanation on a flip chart. Then continue around the room asking other participants to contribute their explanations of that *same* term—"self-starter." Each time, capture that participant's interpretation on the flip chart. Continue this for no more than three of the competencies.

Generally, for a term such as "self-starter," you will get such answers as "thinks well on her feet"; "makes his own decisions"; "never needs to be told what to do"; "always willing to volunteer for assignments without being asked." For a term such as "good human relations," you might hear the following: "gets along well with all levels of the organization"; "cooperative attitude"; "has excellent negotiation skills." Whatever the participants give you, capture it on the flip chart and then say:

"Now you can clearly see that every person has a little different idea of exactly what these broadly based terms actually mean. There is no right or wrong here. The point is, in order to be successful in assessing candidates, you have to be meticulously clear with yourself on what it is that *you* mean. You can put anything here [gesture at the MMM® on the screen] as long as you have a way of scoring it that personally satisfies you.

"Now comes the third and final step in setting up the MMM®—question generation. Which of these definitions [gesture at the explanations of the competencies you wrote on the flip chart] would you like to use as a group exercise?"

Ask for a show of hands. Take a clean transparency or a new flip-chart page and write the definition the group has selected at the top of the sheet.

Then ask the participants to contribute appropriate questions. Capture each question *word for word* on the transparency or flip-chart page. Always ask whether the question contributed is a behavioral or puzzle question.

> *Please note:* Whatever the participants contribute is valid; make no judgments; just utilize whatever they contribute.

When you have four or five questions, select another definition and go through the same procedure.

Before you continue, this might be a good time to suggest that the participants take 2 minutes to review pages 11–14 in their workbooks. Here they will see several examples of the process just completed and realize they will have this to refer to long after the workshop is over.

This might also be an excellent time to remind the participants that the workbook has a number of valuable informational pieces to which they can refer in the future such as:

- Common Errors in Conducting the Interview—pages A-3–A-6
- Interview Questions Listed by Competency Desired—pages A-27– A-61 and on the CD-ROM.
- How to Guarantee Superior Recruitment Assistance from HR or an Employment Agency—pages 23–25
- Questions One Cannot Ask During an Interview—pages 56–57

Now it is time to explain how to develop an MMM® for a *candidate with little or no experience.* Follow the same procedure outlined above, using the information provided below (see also pages 73–75 in the book). Ask participants to take notes on page 15 of their workbooks.

Explain that an MMM® is worthwhile even for an entry-level job or for candidates who have no prior work experience. For example, they can think of school as if it were a job:

- There are goals to be achieved;
- There are deadlines to be met; and
- There are priorities to be sorted out.

Ask the participants to focus on three critical areas: decision making, time management, and confronting problems.

- *Decision Making.* For example, they can ask what candidates did over summer break. What they did is not so important as whether or not they made a conscious choice as to what to do with their time and why. A student might have taken a difficult, physical, but high-paying job to help finance his or her education or a student might have taken a low-paying job in a field in which he or she is interested as a future career possibility.

- *Time Management.* During a four-year college career, a student will have had a year's time (three four-month summers) at his or her disposal. What did he or she do with that time?

- *Confronting Problems.* A third critical item is how students have dealt with problems. For example, if a student was failing a class, did he or she decide to put in extra study time and work with a tutor or did the student drop the class or change majors so that the class was no longer required?

It is a pretty good bet that the behavior of stepping up to challenges in school (or running away from such challenges) will be repeated in the workplace, as will such patterns as choosing play (sports) over handling responsibilities.

Now show the participants how they can incorporate the competency of *motivation* into the MMM® (see pages 75–77 in the book).

Motivation should be a key item on every MMM®. This is because a truly viable candidate must be interested in *this* particular job. When a candidate is interested in a specific field, he or she will:

- Have made efforts to become better at it;

- See a future for himself or herself in that field (have set goals to further his or her depth of knowledge and experience in it); and

- Will evidence strong interest through body language and tone of voice when he or she speaks about challenges undertaken at which he or she succeeded.

You might tell participants:

"You can explore whether or not candidates have tried to expand their knowledge and skills in their particular arena by asking behavioral questions such as 'What have you done recently to become more effective at your current job?' or 'What kinds of circumstances or events have influenced you to learn something new?'

"As candidates talk about their experiences, challenges, and successes, watch for their level of interest. When people are interested in or excited about what they're speaking about, the pupils of their eyes get larger, they lean forward, the speed of their talking increases, and they often become more animated, using hand gestures."

Note Taking During the Interview

(See pages 77–79 in the book.) The last point you need to cover in this section is taking notes during the interview. Here are the points you will want to make:

- Although some note taking is necessary, it should not become a distraction during the interview.

- It's ideal if one can create his or her own shorthand for interviewing purposes so that a single word is sufficient to prompt recall of an exchange.

- During the interview, have only the candidate's resume, your notepad, and the list of twenty to twenty-five prepared questions on your desk. The MMM® with the competencies or characteristics desired should be hidden in the top drawer of your desk.

- As soon as the interview is over, the interviewer should retrieve the MMM® and, using notes, immediately score the candidate on the various competencies.

- This process allows the interviewer to separate information gathering (listening during the interview) from evaluating (after the interview).

You might remind participants:

"The human mind cannot listen and evaluate simultaneously and do a sufficient job at both. Usually it is the listening portion that suffers. This is one of the reasons for inappropriate hires. One of the benefits of using the MMM® strategy is that it allows you to effectively separate those two activities."

At this point, you want to secure the learning regarding the association between the desired competency and appropriate question generation by asking the participants to complete Exercise 2: Question Generation on page 16 in their workbooks (*Suggested Time:* 10 minutes).

After participants have completed and scored the exercise, answer any questions they may have and then summarize this section by reviewing the benefits of using the MMM® that follow.

Benefits of Using the Master Match Matrix®

(See pages 79–86 in the book.) Here you want to discuss the following items:

More Appropriate Candidate/Job Matches.   This is because the focus is on specific expectations and competencies and on how well the candidate fulfills them.

More Competent Listening and Evaluation.   Listening improves because the interviewer does not spend time during the interview thinking up questions (because questions were already generated). Evaluation improves because the interviewer won't be making judgments during the interview (he or she will be gathering data) and because of specific, consistent criteria against which to evaluate each candidate.

> This is an excellent time to ask the class, "What's the most important skill in interviewing?"
>   The correct answer is "listening."

More Effective Recall.   The consistent scoring mechanism of the MMM® allows interviewers to remember which candidates better satisfied each of their requirements. Remember also that this workshop was designed for managers who may have seen one candidate last week, two candidates this week, and who plan to see three candidates next week. How will they remember each one clearly when it comes to making a decision the week after next? The MMM® will help.

No Purchase of Unnecessary Skills.   Because specific requirements are known beforehand, the interviewer won't be unduly impressed by someone's substantial but irrelevant (at least regarding the vacancy) skills.

Ability to Capture the Unique Elements That Determine Success.
The MMM® allows the interviewer to include items that, based on his or her experience, are relevant, but that might not normally appear on a job listing. For example, suppose there was one position that had extremely high turnover. One person, however, had loved the position and remained in it for years. That person had only an eighth-grade education. All the other people who took that job were better educated. The interviewer might therefore want to put "has no more than eighth-grade education" on the MMM®.

Forces a Concentration on the Job Requirements. The focus is on what the interviewer *does* want instead of on the candidate's deficits. In this way, instead of selecting the least objectionable candidate—the one with the fewest deficits—the interviewer matches a candidate's skills against predetermined criteria, thus decreasing the possibility that candidates will be rejected because they don't have a particular skill that may not be a necessary priority for job success.

More Objective (Less Subjective) Process. Each candidate is evaluated using the same basis and criteria, rather than the interviewer evaluating candidates according to their resumes. Evaluating candidates according to their resumes, because they differ from one another, provides a flexible basis for comparison rather than a solid foundation for judgment.

Superior Recruitment Assistance from Human Resources. This method gives HR a far better idea of exactly what is desired in a candidate. A well-crafted MMM® helps them to refer only viable candidates. That means fewer interviews to go through.

It should now be 10:30 a.m. and time for a 15-minute break.

PRE-PLANNING
THE INTERVIEW
(Two-Day Format Only)

Time	Materials
One-Day	Participant Workbook, pages 19–26
NA	
Skip to page 25	Overhead projector
Two-Day	Flip chart
10:45—11:30 am (1st day) (45 min)	Colored markers

BELIEVE IT OR NOT, most managers will go into the task of interviewing totally unprepared to

- Deal effectively with their biases;

- Respond to questions about the company that are important to the candidate;

- Use the interview to obtain information that cannot be acquired any other way; and

- Explain the procedural structures that will organize the candidate's career.

The purpose of this exercise is to raise the participants' awareness of all these items so that they can prepare ahead of time to deal with these issues in a confident and truthful manner. Participants should leave the workshop knowing that interviewing on autopilot instead of on purpose is one sure way to lose a good candidate.

This segment is designed as a group exercise. Assign each table group one page of questions from pages 19–22 of the Participant Workbook.

Tell them they will have 30 minutes to discuss the issues as a group and come to some decision on each question.

After 30 minutes, ask each table group to report its responses and opinions to the entire group. Then, give your input on the issue before moving on to the next group. The points you want to make on each of the questions are shown below.

Know Your Biases

- *Candidate's Attire.* The idea here is that, whatever biases one may have, recognize that they are there and move on. Don't try to fight them because that diverts attention away from listening to the candidate. Biases are OK as long as they are not allowed to control the interviewer's judgment.

- *Candidate's Physical Qualities.* It's important to look at this in a wider context. Attractive people have an easier time in life than do ugly people. It begins in grammar school, where kids can be very cruel to their unattractive classmates. The result may be that the ugly child grows up with poor social skills—either withdrawn or extremely argumentative—and as an adult, a human relations problem at work.

- *First Impressions.* Studies by the Department of Labor and by the Society for Human Resource Management (SHRM) have shown that untrained interviewers make up their minds about a candidate within the first 3 minutes and use the remainder of the interview to reinforce that initial impression. One must keep an open mind. Listen now; evaluate later.

- *Difficult Interviewees.* List what participants say are the most difficult people for them to interview on a flip chart or on a transparency. If the following do not make the list, be sure to add them:

Candidates who are handicapped

Candidates who are shy and refuse to speak

Candidates who won't make eye contact

Candidates who cannot speak the language and who come with an interpreter

Remind the participants that we telegraph our discomfort to the candidate; the object of the interview is for us to make the candidate feel comfortable and not the other way around.

Know Your Company

- *Controversial Topics.* Whatever that topic is, one must be prepared to deal with it confidently, briefly, and positively. The interviewer must be prepared with a strong response.

  Example: Suppose you are a nursing manager in a women's hospital. Your candidate asks you if abortions are done here because "I don't believe in that." Your hospital's services include abortion. You cannot hedge your response nor can you say apologetically, "Well . . . ummm . . . I don't believe in it either but . . . blah, blah, blah." You must answer with conviction, "Yes, we do abortions here. What kind of problem will that create for you?"

- *"Personality" of the Organization.* This is part of "selling" the organization and the opportunity to the candidate. Words such as "old line" and "conservative" will attract a different sort of candidate than will words such as "dynamic" and "unconventional." Telling the truth about the organization's personality is important. The candidate who is comfortable in a dynamic environment might be extremely uncomfortable in a conservative one. Consider the difference between people who work in a bank as opposed to those who work on the floor of the New York Stock Exchange.

- *Salary/Benefits.* Assume the candidate knows more about this topic than the interviewer does. After all, he or she has been looking at other organizations and collecting information. If the interviewer is not 100 percent certain of the facts in this area, he or she must refer the candidate to human resources for those details.

- *Organization's Ranking in Field/Position's Placement in Overall Organization.* The interviewer must be certain to have the answers to these questions; they are frequent queries from the most valuable, sought-after candidates.

Know the Purposes and Pitfalls of the Interview Process

When the group responding to these questions reports out, use the flip chart or transparency and make a list so the participants can see *all* the responses. This is a good time to remind participants of the following:

"Over the years, various studies by the Society for Human Resource Management (SHRM) indicate that 80 percent of the resumes that come across your desk will contain some untruth in them. The most common area of deception occurs in describing job responsibilities. The next involves the dates of employment in various jobs. The other popular area of deception is formal education and degrees."

- *Resume Clarification.* The responses should include specific job results and achievements, career plans and objectives, beliefs and values, self-generated versus company-assigned responsibilities.

- *Information That Can Be Obtained Only Through a Personal Interview.* The responses should include body language, communication skills, ability to think on one's feet, physical (grooming) appearance, energy level, and vigor. Remind participants here that evaluating candidates according to their appearance—with the exception of the grooming issue—can fall into illegal areas.

- *Prior to the Interview.* The responses should include adequate and meticulous preparation; knowing exactly and specifically what is needed and how to "test" for it (with a questioning strategy); that one is ready to devote 100 percent to listening and to leaving the evaluation process for later.

- *Interview Mistakes.* The responses should include talking too much, not being adequately prepared, asking illegal questions, asking dumb questions, telegraphing the answers (which is known as "leading the witness"), not retaining control of the process, using the resume as the basis for the interview, repeating the information on the resume, and not allowing silences to occur.

After the groups report out, mention the following:

"The worst interview mistake is talking too much. The interviewer should speak 20 percent of the time, leaving the candidate to do 80 percent of the talking. Moreover, the content of the interviewer's speech should be confined to comments that encourage the candidate to keep talking. For example, 'yes . . . do go on . . . can you give me an example . . . how exactly did you accomplish that. . . ?'"

Know What the Candidate Might Want to Know

- *Information Interviewer Should Be Prepared to Provide.* Job title, to whom the position reports, salary, how often salaries are reviewed/increased, promotional or advancement opportunities.

- *Answering Candidate Questions.* Once again, the message to the participants is to *be prepared.* They should know the answers to these questions.

The remaining pages in this section of the workbook (pages 23–26) are useful for the participants in preparing to talk with either human resources or an outside employment agency in their quest for candidates. On pages 23–25 is a list of questions and reminders for various topic areas about which HR (or an outside employment agency) would require information to make sound screening decisions. The form on page 26 can be used to provide the information to HR.

You will not be using these forms during the workshop, but you do need to remind the participants that they are there for their use in the future.

Tell the participants (as often as possible—whenever there's an appropriate moment):

> "Although human resources (or the employment recruiter) may be staffed with very perceptive people, they do not know your business as intimately as you do. If you want them to be of substantive assistance to you, you must provide them with as much specific information as possible. The problem is to get that information to human resources (or the employment recruiter) in some sort of format that will make sense to them."

It should now be 11:30 a.m. on the first day of the two-day program and time for a 45-minute lunch break.

TOOLS FOR INTERVIEWING

Time	Materials
One-Day	Transparencies 8-14
10:45—11:45 am (1 hr)	Participant Workbook, pages 27-40
Two-Day	
12:15—1:15 pm (1st day) (1 hr)	Overhead projector
	Two flip charts with easels
	Colored markers
	Blank transparencies

FOR THIS SEGMENT, refer the participants to pages 27–32 of the Participant Workbook and tell them that these are the tools and techniques you will be discussing and that *they are listed in the order in which they will be discussed.* Participants should be encouraged to take notes right in their workbooks in the spaces provided. Listed below are the topics, along with the reference pages in the book. As you go along, provide the participants with illustrative examples.

Time Frame

 (See pages 96-99 in the book.) Place Transparency 8 on the overhead projector.

1. *How long should an interview be?* Forty minutes should be sufficient to interview a professional, technical, or executive candidate; 30 minutes should be sufficient for evaluating candidates for less complex positions such as that of clerical worker.

2. *The "Courtesy" Interview.* This is the first 20 minutes of the interview, during which time the interviewer should try to obtain as much complete information as possible on the most important items of his or her MMM® (items 1–3 possibly). This is where he or she must make a "go" (meaning go on for an additional 20 minutes) or "no go" (meaning the candidate is not viable) decision. The interviewer should use all 20 minutes, even though he or she may form an opinion in the first few minutes.

Say the following to participants to explain why it's important to use all 20 minutes:

"In the first place, it is important that the candidate not feel rushed in and rushed out. Remember that, when we interview, we are also doing something of a PR job for the company. Since it is never easy to find that perfect candidate, we certainly don't want to make the task more difficult for ourselves and for the company by gaining a reputation for being abrupt and impolite.

"Remember that candidates with similar backgrounds probably know one another because they belong to the same professional organizations. Although you may not want this particular candidate because he or she lacks some specific skill, that candidate may know a colleague who is just perfect for your vacancy. Wouldn't it be great if that candidate felt good enough about his or her interviewing experience with you to recommend that a colleague contact you for an interview?"

Explain that it's important to evaluate the candidate based on the responses to questions and not to let a first impression color that evaluation. Say:

"If, after the courtesy interview, you believe that a candidate does not meet the necessary requirements, you should terminate the interview at that point."

3. *The "I'm Interested in Your Candidacy" Interview.* If, after the first 20 minutes, the interviewer believes the candidate does meet the requirements, he or she should continue the interview for an additional 20 minutes, using 10 minutes to sell the job and answer the candidate's questions, the next 5 minutes to delve into another area of inquiry, for example, the candidate's efforts at self-development, and the last 5 minutes to explore a third area of inquiry, perhaps non-work activities, and to wrap up the interview. Tell participants to be sure to inquire about the candidate's goals during the first twenty minutes.

Structured Format

(See pages 87–110 in the book.) Explain that interviewers must make the decision—prior to the interview—about what areas of the candidate's background to cover and how much time to spend on each area.

To make a decision about *what areas to concentrate on,* one must:

- Review the job objectives;
- Clarify the performance expectations;
- Examine the list of competencies desired;
- Look at the MMM®; and last of all
- Glance over the candidate's resume or application.

Selling the company and the job come next. If after 20 minutes of interviewing, the interviewer determines that the candidate meets requirements, he or she should then "sell" the job and the organization. Since this is where most interviewers lose their best candidates, it is critical to introduce this concept of "selling the job and the company" by saying the following:

> "A person will spend eleven thousand days of his or her life between the ages of 21 and 65 at work. That is a staggering amount of time to spend at one single activity in organizations that evidence a decided lack of concern for an individual's personal goals. As an astute interviewer, you want to be certain that no candidate leaves your office feeling that you and the company you represent have that kind of attitude. You want every candidate you spend time with to understand that your organization has a personal stake in every staff person's career success. The unspoken message that you want every candidate to go away with is that you (and your organization) understand that corporate success rests in part upon the personal success of every individual in its employ.
>
> "During the first 20 minutes of the interview, you should endeavor to obtain a clear understanding of what the candidate's long-term career goals are and what he or she is looking for in a job right now *before* you attempt to sell the person on joining your organization.
>
> "An unskilled interviewer will spend far too much time selling the candidate on what the interviewer assumes are the most attractive elements of the job. When this happens, the candidate will leave the interview with the impression that the interviewer (and therefore the company as well) is not truly interested in his or her personal career aspirations. After all, the inter-

viewer never asked the candidate what was attractive in a job or important in terms of his or her career and why.

"When you ask candidates about their goals, they will leave the interview knowing that you are sincerely interested in them and their plans for the future. That being the case, you immediately increase your chances ten-fold that any offer you make will be accepted. This is true even if the candidate has received an offer from another organization at a somewhat higher salary figure."

Discuss the following points about "selling" the job:

- Sell what's appropriate to the candidate. For example, a 22-year-old might be interested in tuition reimbursement, whereas a 50-year-old might be more interested in the retirement plan.

- Ask the candidate what he or she is looking for in terms of personal, career-related benefits.

- Gain additional information about the candidate's aspirations and job preferences by what he or she asks about the organization.

A candidate's interest in *self-development* is always relevant, and the interviewer can pursue the topic by checking the following:

- How much effort has the candidate made to stay up-to-date in his or her field?

- How much initiative has he or she shown in taking on additional tasks or learning new skills as a method of self-development?

Non-work activities can be a clue to a candidate's behavior on the job. Non-work interests often indicate preferences for solitary or collegial pursuits. Discussion of non-work activities may also shed some light on how versatile the candidate is.

CAUTION: Remind participants that they need to be careful about discussing non-work activities. Sometimes this topic area can lead into illegal areas, such as religion or age. For example, a candidate who offers, "I'm president of the Over 50 But We're Nifty Managers' Association" puts you in the awkward and potentially lawsuit-engendering position of knowing the candidate's approximate age.

Structuring Statement

(See pages 91–94 in the book.) A structuring statement is a brief (30 seconds or so) statement that lets the candidate know what to expect. Following is a sample statement:

> "In this company, we make every effort to match people with jobs that draw on their best abilities. We want you to be happy here. We'd like you to gain skills and face challenges that will advance your career goals as well as provide you with appropriate compensation for your efforts. Now, in order for me to do that, I need to know something about your previous job experience, maybe something about any self-development efforts in which you have been involved and something about what you do in your spare time. Suppose you start by telling me about your previous job with ABC Industries."

Using a structuring statement allows the interviewer to accomplish four specific goals:

1. It puts the candidate more at ease by informing him or her of what to expect—how the interview will be managed and the areas to be covered and why.

2. It helps one to retain control of the flow of the interviewing process. By sticking with the topics mentioned in the structuring statement, one is less likely to allow the candidate to get off topic.

3. It saves time. By focusing on the areas to be covered, the interviewer maximizes his or her opportunity to gain relevant information in a limited amount of time.

4. It allows the interviewer to put off answering the candidate's questions when doing so may lead the conversation off topic and keep other more important areas from being covered.

Operant Conditioning

(See pages 94–96 in the book.) Tell the participants the following:

> "Candidates will quickly learn how you want them to behave verbally in the interview. Within the first 5 minutes, if you do most of the talking, candidates will learn that the 'right' way to interview—at least with you—is to listen to you talk. You want them to learn quite the opposite—that the right way to interview is to talk while you listen. This learning process is what is known as operant conditioning."

Explain that the key to training the candidate to do most of the talking is to refrain from speaking, thus showing the candidate that he or she is to do most of the talking. An ideal interviewing strategy is for the interviewer to be speaking about 20 percent of the time, while the candidate speaks 80 percent of the time.

There are at least two options to avoid having to respond to questions from the candidate early on: (1) have an employee or HR representative meet with the candidate just prior to the interview to speak with the candidate or (2) provide some reading material about the organization to the candidate (but not an annual report). Instead, prepare a one- or two-page handout that can be read quickly.

Questioning Strategies

When interviewing, there are four main types of questions: (1) direct questions, (2) open-ended questions, (3) clarifying questions, and (4) self-appraisal questions.

Direct Questions

(See pages 111–117 in the book.) Direct questions ask for a specific piece of information. For examples, "Did you like that job?" or "How many people did you supervise?"

Problems with using direct questions include the following:

- Direct questions require a brief answer, usually "yes" or "no." Therefore minimal information is gained.

- When used back-to-back, the candidate becomes conditioned to provide only brief answers.

- When used back-to-back, direct questions make the interview sound like an interrogation; the exchange does not flow but rather moves along in fits and starts.

- Candidates generally perceive direct questions as threatening and this too reduces the amount of information they give.

Use direct questions under the following circumstances:

- When a specific piece of information such as a date or a number is needed, a direct question may be the best way to get it. *Example:* "When did you get that assignment?" "How many people were involved with you on that project?"

There are two ways to make direct questions more effective:

- Soften them with introductory phrases, making them seem more conversational so that the candidate is less defensive. For example, rather than asking, "How many jobs have you had in the past five years?" say, "I'd be interested to learn how many jobs you've held over the past several years."

- Utilize what is known as the "one-two" approach. Ask a direct question but quickly and immediately follow it with an open-ended question that asks for more information. For example, ask, "Are you the kind of person who likes challenges?" and if the candidate replies, "Yes," follow up with the open-ended question, "How do you like to be challenged?"

Open-Ended Questions

(See pages 117–127 in the book.) Open-ended questions allow for a wide range of answers. Behavioral questions and puzzle questions, which we discussed earlier, are both types of open-ended questions.

Examples: "What is your opinion about...?" "How did you go about making that decision?" "What were your reasons for making that decision?" Open-ended questions begin with the words what, when, where, who, how, and why.

You can say the following to help participants grasp this idea:

"If you listen to the good interviewers on the television or radio, you will find that all of them use open-ended questions. They ask a question and their interviewee-guest talks for 5 minutes trying to answer that one question. Open-ended questions are wonderful because they give you a lot of unanticipated information and because they allow you to hear how the candidate thinks."

Explain that the following are problems with using open-ended questions in the interview:

- They can be time-consuming and

- They give the candidate control of the direction of the interview, at least temporarily.

Example: Suppose the interviewing plan was to spend 10 minutes quizzing the candidate on his experience as a team leader. Suddenly, in response to a question, the candidate hesitates and then responds haltingly, "Well, things didn't work out as well as I had hoped" (this is called "free information"). Immediately the interviewer decides to ask three unplanned questions: (1) "What was your expectation?" (2) "Why do you think things didn't work out as you had hoped?" and (3) "If you were faced with the same circumstances again, what would you do differently?" This is called "branching," and it will lengthen the interview. The information gained from "branching" will probably be well worth the time but, again, it may lead into unplanned areas of discussion.

Explain the following benefits of using open-ended questions:

- They provide more and better quality information;
- They sometimes provide unexpected and extremely useful information;
- They give some insight on how the candidate thinks, perceives, and makes decisions; and
- They are never heard to be as threatening as are direct questions to the candidate.

Say to the participants:

"The most valuable thing you are buying with each and every candidate you hire is what goes on between his or her ears. You want to learn how they think—how they make decisions and how they perceive the world around them. Open-ended questions—especially puzzle questions—will help you do that. Direct questions will not."

Discuss the following interviewing techniques with the group.

Barbara Walters Technique

(See pages 120–122 in the book.) This technique is an ineffective questioning strategy. It consists of asking an open-ended question and then, before the candidate can answer, following up with several more, refining and redefining the initial question with several related but closed-ended questions.

Example: "Where do you see yourself in five years? Does this position fit well into your career plans? Are you interested in expanding your knowledge in this field? Do you think you'd be satisfied doing this work five years from now?"

Say to the group:

"The Barbara Walters Technique is evidence that you have not thought through clearly what it is you wish to ask. Refining the question only confuses the candidate. Most people will answer the question most recently asked—the last in the series—with a "yes" or a "no." Some candidates will select the question they like best from all those asked and answer that one. The problem with this strategy is that the best question in the group—usually the first one—the open-ended one—goes unanswered.

"Ask one question at a time. Remember that if the response you get to a question is insufficient, you can always go back and ask that question again using different words or you can employ the next type of question we will explore, the clarifying question."

Here are the points you want to cover regarding the Barbara Walters technique, emphasizing that the technique is to be avoided:

- This technique dilutes the interviewer's control by allowing the candidate to choose which question to answer;

- To avoid the technique, resist the temptation to immediately clarify a poorly worded question; and

- Allow the candidate to respond to the question (at which point you can ask a follow-up question if necessary) or let the candidate ask you to clarify the question (which you should do using different words).

Clarifying Questions (Probing)

(See pages 122–127 in the book.) Clarifying questions ask for more information or for a more complete response than what the candidate has just provided. A clarifying question can help to ensure that the interviewer understands exactly what the candidate meant and that both are using terms in the same way. Say to the participants:

"Here's what happens in the typical interview. You ask a question and the candidate makes a reasonable response. The response seems to handle your query satisfactorily. So you make three assumptions: (1) the candidate means what he or she says; (2) the candidate is using words and terms the same way that you do; and (3) whatever the candidate has just said represents all the information he or she has on that topic. None of those assumptions may be true. By asking a clarifying question as a follow-up to the candidate's response, you will clean up all those assumptions."

Here are some examples:

Interviewer: "What are you looking for in a job?"
Candidate: "What I'm really looking for is growth."
Interviewer: "Tell me what you mean by 'growth.'" *[clarifying question]*
Candidate: "I want a more important title."

Interviewer: "What was the most difficult task for you on that job?"
Candidate: "There were too many people to deal with."

Interviewer: "Can you give me an example of 'too many people'?" *[clarifying question]*

Candidate: "Well, there were five—my boss and her four reports."

Explain that there are two types of clarifying questions.

1. One asks for a definition. *Example:* "Tell me what you mean by 'managing the team.'"

2. One asks for an illustration. *Example:* "Please give me some specific examples of the strategies you have actually utilized in managing teams."

Use of Clichés by Candidates

Candidates will sometimes use clichés in an attempt to avoid providing specific information. Perhaps they do not have the specific information because their experience is thin to nonexistent. Clarifying questions are useful here because they force candidates to be specific or to admit they have not had that depth of experience. Here are a few examples:

Candidate: "I consider myself to be a real strong team player."

Interviewer: "Tell me what you mean by 'a real strong team player.'"

Candidate: "I keep my mouth shut at team meetings and just go along with whatever the others decide."

Interviewer: "What has been your experience with managing cross-functional teams?"

Candidate: "That's one of my strong suits. People tell me I'm really good at it. It's really quite a rewarding challenge."

Interviewer: "Please give me a specific example of your strategy in dealing with a challenging situation from one of your cross-functional teams."

Say:

"When a candidate makes use of clichés, we begin to suspect he or she may be lying. This is when it pays to notice the candidate's body language and simultaneously get ready to ask several clarifying questions."

Body Language Cues

 (See pages 136–145 in the book.) Place Transparency 9 on the projector and tell the participants:

> "There is one time and one time only when the body language of the candidate is significant, and that is the moment your words die on the air. Then you see before you the candidate's psychological response to your question reflected in his or her body language. Either the candidate liked your question because the answer will make him or her look good or disliked your question because answering it would damage the person's candidacy. Then the candidate responds.
>
> "If you see positive body language, you anticipate hearing a positive response. If you see negative body language, then you anticipate hearing a negative response. The problem comes when you see negative body language but the candidate makes a positive response. Then you know the candidate is not telling the truth. At that point, you should immediately ask a clarifying question."

 Place Transparency 10 on the projector. Following are the points you want to cover:

1. In communication, the majority of the message is conveyed by body language (which includes tone of voice).

2. The two most critical body language gesture issues are

   - *Eye Contact.* Candidates should be making fairly constant eye contact during the interview; if they are looking away, they are likely uncomfortable with the current topic.

   - *Distance Between the Parties.* People tend to move toward things they like and away from things they don't like.

3. Ways to respond to the candidate's body language:

   - Comment on it directly, that is, if the candidate has just moved farther away or averted his or her eyes in response to a question, one might say, "I sense there was some difficulty with . . ." or "My guess is that this decision was made despite your objections."

   - If the candidate seems to be lying (because his or her body language does not match his or her words), follow up with a clarifying question.

Example:

Interviewer: "What has been your experience working with teams?"

Candidate: [head drops forward and down; eyes avert downward to the desk; hands are fiddling with a pen; looks up and smiles] "I really enjoy working with other people on a team."

Interviewer: "Please give me an example from your recent job."

Interviewer's Body Language

(See pages 99, 143–145, and 155 in the book.) Discuss that the interviewer should be careful that his or her body language does not telegraph the interviewer's feelings about a particular response. He or she must project the following positive body language cues:

- Making direct eye contact,
- Leaning slightly forward,
- Keeping hands visible—as much as possible, and
- Maintaining a pleasant facial expression.

Self-Appraisal Questions

(See pages 128–133 in the book.) Self-appraisal questions ask candidates to analyze and evaluate themselves and/or their actions and skills.

Examples: "What do you consider your greatest strengths to be?" "Why do you feel you would be effective in this particular job?"

Say to participants:

"Self-appraisal questions invite the candidate to boast about themselves. Every question implies, 'Please tell me the good things about yourself.' Nowhere do you ask for any problems or weaknesses.

"Untrained interviewers love to ask the question: 'We all have strengths and weaknesses; tell me about your weaknesses.' An astute interviewer would *never* ask that question. It is a bad interviewing strategy. It is asking the candidate to furnish you with a reason for *not* hiring him or her. A candidate would have to be a fool to do that.

"As an astute interviewer, however, you know that candidates come to the interview prepared with two lists. One is an 'A' list, which details all the positive and favorable facts they want to tell you about themselves. You also know that there is a 'B' list that contains all the negative issues the candidate definitely does not want you to know about. You are interested in uncovering this list because this is where problems are likely to surface after hiring.

"Remember that this 'B' list of items is just as foremost in the candidate's mind as is the 'A' list. Since there is no way you can get the candidate to tell you these 'B' items by asking for them directly, what you must do is create a positive and accepting atmosphere where these negative items don't seem so important. In this way, those 'B' list items simply slide into the conversation. It doesn't take much effort for this to happen because these items are already foremost in the candidate's mind. All you need to do is use positive self-appraisal questions in combination with silence."

Using Silence

(See pages 131–133 and 155 in the book.) Explain that it is extremely important to demonstrate the use of the self-appraisal questions in combination with silence to uncover any negative information that the candidate is withholding. Place Transparency 11 on the projector and make the following points:

"Silence is particularly significant at two times: (1) *Immediately after you ask a question.* Here you need to give the candidate time to formulate a response. You should be prepared to wait about 20 seconds before the candidate speaks. Although this may seem like a long time to you, and you may be tempted to refine or follow up on your question, refrain from doing so. Twenty seconds is not a long time for the candidate to consider what the question means and what the best response is. And (2) *Immediately after the candidate's initial response.* Here you want to wait at least 5 seconds before asking another question. This will give the candidate an opportunity to offer other information, frequently from his or her list of negative items that might not otherwise be mentioned.

"Here's the way it works. You ask a self-appraisal question such as 'Which of your many skills and abilities do you think we could use best here in this job?' Now the candidate is faced with three mental decisions to sort out before he or she can respond: (1) What does the interviewer actually want to hear about? (2) How can I put myself in the best light when I respond? and (3) What words and phrases should I use so I express myself intelligently? Twenty seconds is not a great deal of time in which to accomplish all that mental activity. Be patient. Eventually you will get the candidate's carefully crafted and positive response from the 'A' list. [Point to the appropriate place on Transparency 11.]

"When the candidate has finished speaking, say nothing. Continue to give the candidate direct eye contact. Telegraph with your body language the silent message that you are waiting to hear the rest of the candidate's story. After a 5-second period of silence, the candidate will blurt out some item from his or her 'B' list." [Point to the appropriate place on Transparency 11.]

Encouragements

(See pages 133–134 in the book.) Say the following:

"Sometimes the candidate will not offer additional information after the 5-second waiting period. In this case, you can offer some encouragement, of which there are three types: one- and two-word comments such as 'yes,' 'good,' and 'uh-huh'; direct requests for elaboration, such as 'I'd like to hear more about that' and 'Please continue'; or body-language cues such as nodding your head or making a small sweeping motion toward yourself with your hand."

Now would be a good time to review with the participants the various types of questions by putting Transparency 12 on the projector and asking the participants to complete Exercise 3 on page 33 in the Participant Workbook (*Suggested Time:* 5 minutes). After everyone has completed the exercise and the scoring, answer any questions the exercise might have generated. Then continue on to the topic of Listening Skills. Refer participants to page 30 and 31 for note taking.

Listening Skills

(See pages 145–150 in the book.) This is a critical topic in your presentation because listening is the most important skill in interviewing. Introduce this topic by placing a blank transparency on the projector and saying:

"Most interviewers talk too much and spend far too much mental time concentrating on question generation while the candidate is sitting in front of them, instead of listening to the candidate's responses. The only time you can listen to the candidate is when he or she is in front of you speaking. You learn nothing when you do all the talking. The candidate is on stage here, not you. You are merely the audience."

Teaching Strategy

Refer to the diagram model entitled "Active Listening Skills." As you make the speech and detail the points listed below, draw this model on a blank transparency. Participants need to see this model in their minds' eye every time they interview. It emphasizes the fact that listening is not about judging (yes, that was good; no, that was bad) nor is it about evaluating (this might be a good skill for the job; we really can't use that skill here). Listening in the interview is about gathering data and asking questions that encourage the candidate to keep talking so that we can continue listening.

ACTIVE LISTENING SKILLS MODEL

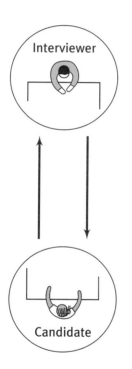

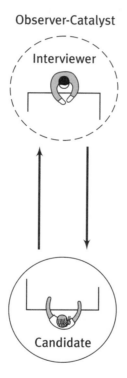

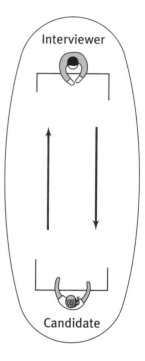

Tell the participants the following, illustrating with the model as directed:

"When we speak to other people in any situation, not just an interview, we come into that exchange with our mental set of the moment and they come with theirs. [*On the blank transparency, draw the two circles on the left–hand side of the model in the figure, along with the arrows. The top one represents the interviewer; the bottom one represents the candidate. Label them accordingly.*]

"For example, let's say that it is 4:00 p.m. Human resources has sent you three candidates to interview before you leave for the day. You look at your watch and say to yourself, 'If I give them each the 20-minute special—the courtesy—maybe I can get out of here by 5:00.' So your mental set is about getting through this interviewing thing as quickly as possible. The candidates, however, really want to work for your company and are very nervous about the interview because human resources told them you were the decision maker. So the candidates' mental set is about anxiety and making a good impression.

"Now, if you are a superior interviewer, which you certainly will be after this workshop, you participate in this interviewing conversation without your current mental set but recognizing and accepting the candidate's mental set. [*Now draw the middle set of circles with arrows, except that the circle representing the interviewer—the top one—should be sketched in with a broken and light line.*]

"For example, suppose the first candidate is a very recent graduate and this is his first interview. He is nervous beyond words. You know this because beads of sweat are dripping off his brow and damp marks are appearing on the underarm portion of his jacket. So you say to the candidate, 'You know I used to get nervous over interviews myself, but all I'm going to do is ask you a few questions about your favorite courses, what you'd like to do here, and maybe something about how you spent your summers, and that's it.' Immediately the candidate visibly relaxes.

"It may be that you have never been as nervous about anything as the candidate is. However, you saw what the candidate's mind-set was at the moment and you accepted it. Moreover, you did not let your own mind-set get in the way. What you did was take the role of observer-catalyst. [*Write the word 'observer-catalyst' at the top of the broken circle representing the interviewer.*]

"Playing this role is exceedingly difficult to do because we are deeply affected by the presence of the person who seats him- or herself in front of us.

"For example, say the candidate is wearing a hearing aid. We automatically raise our voices ten decibels. Why do we do that? Well, we are trying to help the candidate to hear. But he or she doesn't need our help; he or she is wearing a hearing aid.

"Think of it this way. The candidate is playing tennis and we are the backboard, not another tennis player. Our only function is to keep the conversation going, not by participating in it but rather by encouraging the other person to continue talking so that we can listen.

"There are three tools that will assist you in doing just that: the *parrot,* the *paraphrase,* and the *feedback of feelings.* When you make use of any of those three tools, candidates will believe that you actually share their mind-sets. [*Now draw a large oval on the right side of the transparency. Put the word 'interviewer' inside the oval at the top and the word 'candidate' at the bottom inside the oval with the communication arrows.*]

"For example, let's go back to the nervous recent grad. As soon as you said, 'I used to get nervous over interviews myself,' the candidate immediately settled down because he was probably thinking, 'Gee, this person really understands what I'm going through.' Once that happens, the candidate no longer sees you as a judge and a critic. His willingness to communicate expands and you will be more likely to get open, honest, unmonitored communication."

Here again are the points you want to make:

1. Each person comes to an exchange with a particular *mind-set* based on his or her feelings, attitudes, and circumstances.

2. A good interviewer tries to put his or her own mind-set aside and focus on the candidate.

3. Good interviewing technique requires one to decipher the candidate's mind-set and then say whatever is appropriate so that the candidate believes that the interviewer shares his or her context, that is, appears empathic or understanding, thus putting the candidate more at ease and making him or her more likely to be forthcoming.

4. By using the verbal tools of the parrot, the paraphrase, and the feedback of feelings, the interviewer encourages the candidate to be open, to speak more openly, and to communicate more honestly and unguardedly.

Some examples of these techniques are given below. Go over them with the group.

Parrot

(See pages 127–128 and 147–148 in the book.) To parrot, the interviewer repeats back to the candidate his or her last word or phrase in a questioning tone, indicating the need for further clarification. This strategy is always heard by the candidate as if it were a clarifying question.

Example:
Candidate: "... and I found all of that really unethical."
Interviewer: "Unethical?"

Candidate: "Yes! I think when a manager doesn't care if his or her people leave work early, it's like letting them steal from the company."

Paraphrase

(See pages 145-155 in the book.) With this technique, the interviewer puts what he or she thinks the candidate has said in his or her own words and asks whether that is right. The paraphrase usually begins with the words, "As I understand it, you're telling me that. . . . Is that right?"

Feedback of Feelings

(See pages 145-152 in the book.) With this technique, the interviewer responds to the candidate's body language rather than to his or her words, telling the candidate what he or she thinks is going on. The candidate corrects interpretations that are wrong.

Example:

Candidate: "He was, well, ummm, I guess you might say he was just a difficult person." [Candidate averts eyes, shakes head in a "no" movement, and sighs heavily.]

Interviewer: "Sounds as if all your efforts to make the relationship work failed."

Candidate: "Yes."

Interviewer: "Tell me about it."

Notice that the interviewer did not respond to the candidate's words but rather to what the interviewer thought he or she saw in the candidate's body language—a sense of frustration.

Suppport/Confront

(See pages 150–152 in the book.) When an understanding atmosphere has been created, candidates will sometimes divulge information that they may wish they had not. The interviewer can often tell this by body language; the candidate may pull away or cover his or her mouth with a hand. The support/confront technique is a way of assuring candidates that their disclosure hasn't necessarily hurt their candidacy and of encouraging them to continue speaking.

For example, say someone is being interviewed for a customer service job. The interviewer has already told this candidate that about 10 percent of the customers that she will have to deal with may be unpleasant or even abusive when the following exchange happens:

Interviewer: "What did you like the least about that particular job?"

Candidate: "One of the things I really hate is dealing with nasty people on the phone." [Suddenly the candidate's hand goes to her mouth, she moves back in her chair, she then crosses her arms across her chest, and looks at the interviewer with her lips pursed together in a thin line.]

Interviewer: "Everyone on the customer service staff would agree with you that dealing with nasty people is far and away the toughest part of the job. Tell me about the worst customer you've ever had to deal with" [support/confront statement followed by a behavioral question].

Candidate: [arms uncross; she smiles and leans forward] "There was this one time when shipping had really messed up this customer's order. . . ."

In order to secure the learning from this section, ask the participants to complete page 34, Exercise 4, in their workbooks (*Suggested Time:* 5 minutes). After the participants have completed the exercise and the scoring, respond to any questions the exercise may have generated.

Then ask the participants to move on to pages 35–40, Exercises 5 and 6 in the Participant Workbook (*Suggested Time:* 20 minutes) so that they can clearly understand the importance of listening to the candidate's responses while watching his or her body language and following up appropriately. Once again, after the participants have completed the exercise and the scoring, respond to any questions the exercises may have generated.

Broken Record Technique

(See pages 165–168 in the book.) Refer participants to page 31 in their workbooks as you begin the discussion. This technique can be used when interviewing a candidate who is trying to avoid answering a question. The technique consists of simply repeating a question again and again until the candidate responds to the question. Rarely is it necessary to repeat the question more than once or twice. The candidate will quickly get the idea that he or she cannot avoid responding.

Example:

Interviewer: "If I were to ask your previous employer for a reference, what might she most likely tell me about you?"

Candidate: "Well, actually I think she's no longer with the company."

Interviewer: "If I were to ask your previous employer for a reference, what might she most likely tell me about you?"

Candidate: "I think she retired and went to California to look after a sick parent."

Interviewer: "If I were to ask your previous employer for a reference, what might she most likely tell me about you?"

Candidate: "Well, she wouldn't say anything very positive."

Interviewer: "If I were to ask your previous employer for a reference, what might she most likely tell me about you?"

Candidate: "She'd tell you I was asked to leave because of bookkeeping irregularities."

Opening and Closing the Interview

(See pages 87–88, 91–94, 99, and 109–110 in the book.) Remind participants to take notes on page 32 in their workbooks. Here are the points you want to make:

- The astute interviewer always begins the interview with some sort of a structuring statement (1) to let the candidate know how he or she intends to manage the exchange, (2) to let the candidate know what to expect in terms of questions, and (3) to let the candidate know what will be accomplished in the interview.

- When closing an interview one should (1) thank the candidate for his or her time, (2) express how much you enjoyed speaking with him or her, and (3) let the candidate know what to expect in terms of the follow-up process.

  Example: "Thank you for coming by today to speak with us. I certainly have enjoyed talking with you. I still have several more candidates to interview, but you should be hearing from us within the next two weeks. In the meantime, if you have any additional questions, please do not hesitate to call me." [Give business card. Shake hands. Walk candidate to the door.]

If you are using the one-day format, it should now be 11:45 a.m. and time for a lunch break.

If you are using the two-day format, continue on with the next segment.

ADVANCED QUESTIONING CHALLENGES
(Two-Day Format Only)

Time	Materials
One-Day	Transparencies 13–14
NA	Participant Workbook, pages 41–46
Skip to page 61	
Two-Day	Colored markers
1:15—2:00 pm (1st day)	Two flip charts with easels
(45 min)	Blank transparencies

WHAT FOLLOWS IN THIS SEGMENT are some of the finer points of questioning strategy. Since these points will be covered by lecture, it is important that you provide the participants with examples of each. Tell participants that the main points of the discussion are listed on pages 41 and 42 of their workbooks.

Getting the Shy Candidate to Speak

(See pages 187–188 in the book.) Explain that, in this situation, the interviewer uses short questions that require very long answers. And while the candidate is responding, the interviewer must sit quietly and listen without interrupting. Say that three types of questions can be used.

1. Ask for a list of something. *Example:* "Give me a list of all the things you do on your job."

2. Request an explanation of a procedure. *Example:* "Walk me through the procedure you used for justifying the addition of a staff member."

3. Ask the candidate to describe a typical day. *Example:* "Tell me what a typical day looks like for you from the very start until you leave at the end of the day."

Tell participants that it is critical to stay away from direct questions altogether because they require only brief answers, thus making it even more difficult to get the shy candidate to talk.

Making Questions More Productive

(See pages 159–161 in the book.) Cover the four ways to make questions more productive:

1. Use numbers to make the question more quantitative. *Example:* "What are the three most important things you are looking for in a job?"

2. Ask the candidate to compare and contrast something. *Example:* "What do you think are the major differences between your priorities for this job as compared to those in your previous job?"

3. Ask the candidate to analyze and evaluate something. *Example:* "If you could design an effective absentee and tardiness policy, what would it include and why?"

4. Ask the candidate to assume a different point of view. *Example:* "If you were a customer, what skills and qualities would you expect to encounter in a good customer-service person?"

Making the Interview More Conversational

(See pages 161–165 in the book.) Here are the points you want to make.

1. The interviewer can make queries into statements. This technique can increase the candidate's comfort level because the interview will seem less like an inquisition.

2. Encouragements such as "yes," "good," or "uh-huh" can be used. This technique conveys interest in what the candidate has to say. Even more intense phrases such as "unbelievable" or "wow!" may also be used.

3. The interviewer can start sentences for the candidate to complete as a means of encouraging longer comments. Examples would be: "So what you realized was . . ." or "So the implication was . . ." or "And in the end. . . ."

Dumb Questions

(See pages 172–176 in the book.) Introduce this topic by placing Transparency 13 on the projector and telling the participants the following:

> "Dumb questions are those which have obvious 'right' answers and those whose only function is to take up space in the silence. With proper preparation, these dumb questions should never make it into your interviewing strategy. The problem is that such questions have a tendency to creep in no matter how careful you are. If you find dumb questions creeping into your interview, the best thing to do is stop for a moment, consider what information you need, then very deliberately ask a behavioral or clarifying question as a strategy for continuing on."

Say that there are four main types of dumb questions:

1. Questions that telegraph the desired response. *Example:* "This job requires some experience with budget administration. How are you at handling budgets?"

2. Questions that offer a choice of responses except that there really is no sane choice if the candidate wants the job. *Example:* "Are you a self-starter or do you require constant prodding in order to get anything done?"

3. Questions where the answers, although obvious, cannot be checked for truthfulness. *Example:* "Do you consider yourself to be a person who is careful with confidential information?"

4. Questions that serve no purpose except to fill the silence and allow the interviewer additional mental time for question generation. *Example:* "So you'll have no problem juggling and integrating various priorities?"

Responding to Evasion Tactics

(See pages 44, 141–142, and 165–172 in the book.) To begin this topic, place Transparency 14 on the projector and tell the participants:

> "Inevitably in the process of interviewing, you will ask candidates questions they do not wish to answer. Perhaps it is because they fear the response will impact negatively on their candidacy. Maybe they are unprepared for your query or do not have an appropriate response and need additional time to conjure up something applicable. Whatever the reason, you do *not* get an answer to your question. You get something else.

"As you might imagine, in order to successfully negotiate around this type of verbal trap, an interviewer must exercise his or her best listening skills."

Here are the points you want to cover regarding candidate evasion and manipulation tactics:

An effective strategy involves listening and hearing that a question was not answered and immediately following up with an appropriate question that lets the candidate know he or she *must* respond.

The most common candidate question-evasion tactics and examples of each follow. Go over them with participants.

1. Utilizing the interviewer's words to make up a related question that was not asked and answering that question instead. *The remedy* is to use the "Broken Record" technique.

    Interviewer: "How have you utilized goal setting as a management technique?"

    Candidate: "I certainly believe in goal setting as a management technique. It's a great tool."

    Interviewer: "How have you utilized goal setting as a management technique?"

    Candidate: "As a matter of fact, I tried to get my boss interested in recommending that strategy to the entire division."

    Interviewer: "How have you utilized goal setting as a management technique?"

2. Asking the interviewer a laundry-list question as a clarifying question in the hopes that the interviewer will "give away" the correct response. *The remedy* is to re-ask the question using different words or to respond "both" or "all."

    Interviewer: "Tell me about the most challenging decision you've had to make."

    Candidate: "Do you mean at this job as a division manager or at one of my previous jobs as a department manager?"

    Interviewer: "Both."

3. When presented with a choice of responses (the laundry-list question), the candidate asserts that both choices are acceptable. *The remedy* is to ask the candidate for an illustrative example of each choice.

    Interviewer: "Do you prefer to work in groups as a team member or would you rather work alone as an individual contributor?"

    Candidate: "I actually like both modes equally well."

Interviewer: "Please give me an example of your experience in each mode. I'd be interested to learn what the specific project was and how you felt about the outcome."

4. Refusing to answer the question by side-stepping the issue with some plausible excuse. *The remedy* is to agree that the candidate's excuse is reasonable but to insist that he or she tackle the problem anyway.

Interviewer: "How would you handle a very talented, valuable employee who was habitually and seriously late?"

Candidate: "I'm not at all familiar with your company's rules about that sort of thing and how strictly those rules are enforced."

Interviewer: "I can appreciate that. Nevertheless, I'd like to hear your take on that sort of thing since it's a common management problem."

It is now time to secure the learning by asking the participants to test themselves by completing pages 43–46 (Exercises 7 and 8) in their workbooks (*Suggested Time:* 5 minutes for Exercise 7 and 10 minutes for Exercise 8). After everyone has completed both exercises and the scoring, ask for and respond to any questions the group may have.

At this point, it will be 2 p.m. on the first day of the two-day session and time for a break.

ADVANCED INTERVIEWING STRATEGIES (Two-Day Format Only)

Time	Materials
One-Day	Participant Workbook, pages 47–51
NA	Colored markers
Skip to page 61	Overhead projector
Two-Day	Two flip charts with easels
2:15—3:00 pm (1st day) (45 min)	

THE TOPICS IN THIS SESSION REPRESENT some of the finer points of interviewing: resume analysis, record keeping, rapid screening strategies, "round-robin" or team interviewing, interviewing by phone, and hiring professionals. Have participants take notes, starting on page 47 of their workbooks.

Resume Analysis

(See page 80 in the book.) Begin this session by saying the following:

> "Studies done by SHRM (the Society for Human Resource Management) have shown that 80 percent of the resumes that come across your desk will contain some untruth in them. The most common area of deception occurs in describing job responsibilities. The next involves the dates of employment in various jobs. The other popular area of deception is formal education and degrees. Although the interviewing strategy presented in this workshop is designed to make the candidate's resume pretty much irrelevant, you (and your HR representative) should be aware of a few issues.

"First, a resume is a sales and marketing piece designed by the candidate depicting himself or herself in the most advantageous light possible. A resume, therefore, may contain many inaccuracies such as the following:

- 'Have familiarity with all types of platforms.' (In actuality, the candidate read a book that described the various platforms. He or she has experience working with only one.)
- 'Worked closely with the director of software engineering.' (The candidate's cubicle was twenty feet away from the director's office.)
- 'Assumed responsibility for managing the office in the boss's absence.' (The candidate answered the boss's phone while the boss was otherwise engaged or out of the immediate area.)
- 'Extensive experience with project management.' (The candidate was a team member on an extensive project where he or she observed someone else handling the responsibility of project management.)

"Human resources requires a resume to make certain the candidate has the background, skill sets, and knowledge specified by you as the hiring manager.

"A resume is built around the candidate's professional history. The hiring manager (that's you) is interested in the candidate's *potential*—the ability to successfully utilize what he or she knows in your work environment.

"The traditional approach for interviewing has been to utilize the candidate's resume as the foundation for the interviewing conversation. Since every resume is different, this method uses a variable and inconsistent foundation as the basis for the interview.

"The strategy advanced in this workshop involves the use of the Master Match Matrix® as the foundation for the interviewing conversation. It is a firm and stable base built upon the needs and requirements of the position as seen by you, the hiring manager, rather than the candidate's marketing piece or advertisement."

Record Keeping and Related Paperwork

(See pages 231–244 in the book.) Under this topic, you want to cover the following points:

- Everything to do with hiring is subject to judicial review—*everything.*

- Resumes should be kept on file for twelve months.

- The only marks that should be made on the resume by the interviewer are the date of the interview and the initials of the interviewer.

- Any notes taken during the interview should be recorded on a separate piece of paper and filed away in a personal file—*not* with the resume. A subpoena will bring forth all official paperwork but not the personal files of the interviewer.

- The candidate has the "right of disclosure," which means that he or she has the right to see anything on the interviewer's desk that relates to his or her interview. Therefore, if the candidate sees the interviewer writing notes on the resume (or on anything else), he or she can ask to see what the interviewer has written. The interviewer must show that information to the candidate. Negative comments can be grounds for suit.

Explain that most organizations have an official employment application that contains a paragraph that states, "I understand that if any of the statements I have made here are found to be false, that will be grounds for instant termination." Most candidates will object to completing that application form, claiming that all that information is already on their resume. If that is the case, the interviewer can take the following steps:

1. Make certain that each candidate signs the disclaimer paragraph on the employment application.

2. Have the candidate draw a diagonal line across the front of the application form and write "see resume attached" on that line.

3. Then ask the candidate to complete the name, address, and phone number information at the top of the application form. This effectively ties the two documents together legally.

Explain that an "Offer of Employment Letter" is a legal document (see pages 234–237 in the book) and as such should be prepared by human resources and reviewed by a lawyer.

If a "Non-Compete Agreement" or an "Employment Contract" (see pages 232–234 in the book) is to be a part of the hiring process, it should be reviewed by a lawyer before being presented to the candidate. Non-compete agreements have no legal teeth unless they are a part of the hiring process and "reasonable" in their restrictions.

Example: Extending for no more than one year and only within a defined geographical area such as "Greater Atlanta area" rather than "the State of Georgia."

Rapid Screening Technique

Say that sometimes the interviewer may need to use a rapid screening technique, which consists of the following steps, which you may wish to write on the flip chart:

1. Construct an MMM® of four to five requirements that can be easily determined by examining a resume or by utilizing a few direct questions over the phone. *For example:* three years of general sales and customer service experience; college graduate or associate degree; valid drivers license; at least one year of experience supervising other sales personnel; and recent industry experience.

2. Inform HR or your clerical assistant that the only candidates you want to see are those with at least four out of the five requirements indicated on your brief MMM®.

3. In this way, HR or the clerical assistant can do the screening for you, either by examining the resumes or by conducting brief screening interviews over the telephone.

Round Robin and Team Interviews

(See pages 78–79 and 144–145 in the book.) Here are the points you want to cover:

- In *round robin* interviewing, the candidate is interviewed separately and in private, one-on-one, with each member of the interviewing team.

- In *team* interviewing, the candidate is interviewed by several people simultaneously.

- Only one type of candidate (the "power person") does well with group interviews; other candidates feel under such pressure and strain that it is doubtful that an accurate, reliable picture of the candidate will emerge.

- Round robin interviewing provides much better results than team interviewing. Since each person's interviewing style varies, each may see different facets of the candidate. In this way, the amount of data gathered on a given candidate is enriched.

- The more people who are involved in the interviewing process, the more time-consuming it will be. More time will also be required to reach a decision. If the candidate's particular skills are in demand, the company could well lose him or her to a competitor while a "team" is attempting to reach consensus.

- If several individuals are going to be involved in the interviewing process, they should meet beforehand to design the MMM® *as a group* so everyone is in agreement as to the qualities desired in the successful candidate. This will prevent the problem mentioned above.

- The next step is to divide the MMM® topic areas among the interviewers to ensure that the candidate will *not* be asked the same questions from each member of the team. If everyone asks the same questions, the candidate will "learn" what the preferred answers are, thus increasing the chance that later interviewers will form a more favorable opinion of the candidate than may actually be warranted.

- After all the interviews are over, the interviewing team should get together, pool their findings, and make a decision.

Interviewing by Telephone

Here are the points you want to cover:

- Telephone interviewing tends to lend itself to heavy use of direct questions. Extreme caution and awareness must be used to avoid this tendency so that the interviewer can gain sufficient information from which to make a sound hiring decision.

- Telephone interviewing is mainly a one-dimensional form of communication because the interviewer misses all the body language cues and the physical reaction to the "presence" of the other person.

- If the situation requires that the interview be conducted by telephone, the interviewer must take the following steps:

  1. Prepare questions ahead of time to prevent the use of direct questions.

  2. Close his or her eyes when the candidate is responding to a question in order to shut out all other distracting incoming data. This will make it easier for the interviewer to concentrate 100 percent on listening to what is being said and how it is being said.

  3. Listen for tone of voice, pace, pauses, and changes in tone of voice, pace, or volume (loud versus soft).

  4. Try to visualize what the candidate might be doing with his or her body language as he or she responds. The interviewer must try to match the candidate's vocal changes with appropriate body cues.

Hiring Professionals

Ask everyone to turn to workbook page 49. Say to the group:

"Professionals are defined as those persons having specialized educational backgrounds and/or degrees (such as engineers or accountants) or those with substantial, extensive experience in a particular field. Their backgrounds qualify them for greater levels of salaried compensation.

"Others are defined as those persons whose career backgrounds are much more common in the marketplace (such as clerical personnel, trainees of various kinds, and general administrators). Their backgrounds are less specialized and focused, perhaps because these candidates have not yet set themselves on a firm career path. These persons may be paid on an hourly basis.

"The differences between these two groups of candidates center around the way each responds to questioning. In other words, 'professionals' will respond differently than will 'other' candidates. Therefore, when preparing an MMM® and queries, the interviewer first must sort out in his or her own mind which kind of candidate is sought to fill the vacancy and prepare response expectations accordingly."

Tell the participants that there is a very complete outline of the significant differences between professionals as candidates and other types of candidates on pages 49–50 in their Participant Workbooks. Offer the participants several examples such as those provided below:

Interviewer: "What's important to you in a job?"
Professional: "That I keep my skills challenged, up-to-date, and growing."
Other: "That I work with nice people on interesting projects."

Interviewer: "How do you know when you've done a good job?"
Professional: "A lot of that is internalized. It's always about doing my personal best no matter what the circumstances. I guess I'm my toughest critic when it comes to that."
Other: "I receive feedback from my boss or my co-workers or a customer."

Interviewer: "How does this position fit into your overall career plan?"
Professional: "Since I've already had experience doing zzz, I expect to gain a lot of experience here doing xxx."
Other: "I'm hoping this job will help me become more effective at what I do and maybe pick up a few new skills."

Interviewer: "I'd be interested to learn why you left your last job."
Professional: "The work was no longer challenging."
Other: "There was no opportunity for growth."

Make the following points regarding hiring professionals:

- Hiring "professionals" is one of management's most important decisions because the person will shape the job, not the other way around. *Example:* Think about the difference between a production worker and a sales manager.

- Look for the following in a "professional" candidate:
  - Positive attitude and a good disposition—especially if going into a leadership position;
  - Proof of high technical or managerial performance;
  - Ability to enhance group performance;
  - Initiative taking and independent thinking;
  - Ability to learn (doesn't act as if he or she has all the answers);
  - Potential for development and renewal;
  - High probability of retention; and
  - Creativity.

- Issues that have NO bearing on later job success of a professional include:

  - Grade point average during college;

  - Extracurricular activities during college;

  - Percentage of school cost earned during college;

  - Appearance at the interview;

  - Stated goals; and

  - Prestige of school attended.

- Issues that have GREAT bearing on later job success:

  - Channel of recruitment (how the resume got to your desk);

  - First assignment (they have high expectations and must be challenged right away);

  - Past technical or managerial performance (references);

  - Some generalist skills;

  - Age and experience (older is better than younger);

  - "Nice" personality (especially if going to be a team member or in a leadership role); and

  - Locus of control (believe they control their own destiny).

- Issues pertaining to retention of professionals:

  - Young people are most likely to leave;

  - Government hires are more likely to remain; and

  - Well-performing professionals will leave an organization when there is (1) no chance for self-actualization (growth, challenge, promotion, or learning) (2) when secrecy exists in the organization, (3) when the work is not challenging, or (4) when they do not like the way they are being managed (usually too much structure).

It should now be 3:00 p.m. on the first day of the two-day session.

VIDEO FEEDBACK PROCEDURE
(Two-Day Format Only/First Day)

Time	Materials
One-Day	Videotape
NA	Video playback unit
Skip to page 61	Overhead projector
Two-Day	Colored markers
3:00—4:00 pm (1st day) (1 hr)	Two flip charts with easels
	Blank transparencies

For the First Day Viewing

Introduce this segment to the participants by saying:

"We are now going to watch a series of video clips of interviews (from either previous classes you have facilitated or, if this is your first time presenting this workshop, a commercially produced tape purchased from The Corporate Training Shop). I will play one clip and stop the machine so that all of you can analyze what occurred in the film. You want to notice such things as body language; dumb questions asked by the interviewer; whether the candidate actually answered the question asked; whether the interviewer followed up the candidate's responses appropriately; any use of the special tools we reviewed such as broken record, the clarifying question, the parrot, the self-appraisal question, and so on; any use of silence; and whether the interviewer maintained the observer-catalyst position. Although you may find it helpful to take notes, I would prefer that you simply concentrate 100 percent on the film—on what you see and what you hear."

Teaching Strategy

Start the videotape. Stop the tape after each vignette and ask the participants to comment on what they saw going on in terms of what they have learned so far. Make sure that, within the hour that you are engaged in this activity, everyone has a chance to comment.

Whatever the participants say about the videotape is just fine. You can add your comments as well—but only after the participants make theirs.

The purpose here is for the participants to begin the processes of

- Listening (and watching) critically;

- Interviewing on purpose instead of on autopilot;

- Recognizing how the different strategies work in actual practice; and

- Perceiving the errors as they happen.

PARTICIPANT INSTRUCTIONS FOR ROLE-PLAY ACTIVITY

Time	Materials
One-Day	Participant Workbook, pages 53–54
12:30—1:00 pm (30 min)	Colored markers
Two-Day	Two flip charts with easels
4:00—4:15 pm (1st day) (15 min)	Blank transparencies

DURING THIS PORTION OF THE WORKSHOP, the participants will be working on their own to prepare an MMM® and a set of ten appropriate questions to use later on when they role play the part of "interviewer." The purpose of this exercise is for the participants to see how all the pieces and parts of the interviewing process actually do fit together.

Refer the participants to page 53 in the Participant Workbook. Read the instructions on page 53 and have the participants follow along with you. Emphasize that the vacancy for which they will be preparing the MMM® and for which they will be interviewing candidates is that position for which they most often interview in their jobs. If they do this preparation work well, they will be able to leave the workshop with a complete MMM® and selection of appropriate questions to use the next time they interview.

- Tell the participants that there is an MMM® shell for them to use on page 54 of their Participant Workbook. They may also use the forms on pages 6 and 7 as well (also available on the CD-ROM).

- In addition, let participants know that they can use any question found in the list of Interview Questions Listed by Competency Desired beginning on page A-27 of the Participant Workbook (also available on the CD-ROM), as well as any other questions they like using or have developed themselves.

- The only rule is that each of the selected questions—when answered—MUST assist in the scoring of the MMM®.

- Everyone will need a copy of *his or her own* resume to use during the role play. Out-of-date resumes will work just fine. If a participant tells you he or she does not have a resume available, have that person take some of the preparation time to prepare a *brief* resume (just some information about his or her present job and a little about their educational background).

- The actual live role-play interviews will be about 5 minutes long so a vast amount of preparation is unnecessary. The role-play activity is not brain surgery. Its only purpose is to get the participants comfortable with the process and experience how all the pieces of preparation fit together into an effective whole.

- Completing this assignment should take no more than 30 minutes.

For the one-day format, participants will be completing the interviewing preparation assignment during the session from 12:30 to 1:00 p.m.

For the two-day format, participants will complete the interviewing preparation assignment as *homework* on the evening of the first day.

LEGAL RESTRICTIONS
AND RELATED ISSUES*

Time	Materials
One-Day	Participant Workbook, pages 55–62
2:15—3:00 pm (45 min)	Overhead projector
Two-Day	Colored markers
8:30—9:15 am (2nd day) (45 min)	Two flip charts with easels
	Blank transparencies

THE LEGAL RESTRICTIONS on interviewing have been with us for more than twenty years now, so most of your participants are probably quite knowledgeable about the topic. The most efficient way of handling this topic, therefore, would be to *devote most of the time in this segment to a question-and-answer session.* Begin, however, by covering these basic points:

- Any measurement or parameter used to evaluate a candidate in employment selection is subject to legal review and regulations—*everything.*

- When it comes to Equal Opportunity legislation, the interviewer represents the company, which means that the company is liable for any illegal errors the interviewer makes.

*Note: Because of the two-day schedule, this section and the next one are in reverse order for the one-day workshop. If you are leading the one-day workshop, skip to the role-play activity on page 69, do that section first, and then return to this section before continuing with People Reading on page 81.

- One must treat all candidates equally. If you would not ask the question of a male candidate, then do not ask it of a female candidate.

- The interviewer must focus on the candidate's skills and qualifications as they relate to the job and ask nothing about the candidate's personal life.

- While asking about a candidate's hobbies can give another dimension to the person, this topic area can put the interviewer into legal difficulty, depending on the candidate's responses.

- A candidate can allege anything. The employer must prove that it did not happen. Therefore, when interviewing, one must stay away from the topic areas listed on page 55 of the workbook.

- The purpose of all Equal Opportunity legislation is to ensure that employers do not unnecessarily limit the pool from which they select their candidates.

- The word "restricted" on page 55 of the workbook was very carefully chosen because there are parts of this information that are not considered discriminatory areas.

Questions One Can and Cannot Ask During an Interview

After making the general comments above, tell participants to take a moment to review pages 56–57 in their workbooks and to let you know if they have any questions.

Be prepared to explain all of the issues/topics raised on pages 56–57 of the workbook. The topic areas that tend to generate the most questions are listed and explained on the next page.

Topic Area	Restriction and Explanation
Availability for Saturday and Sunday work	It is illegal to ask about religion. If weekend work is required, say so in the job description and tell the candidate, "This job requires Saturday and Sunday work." The law states that once hired, a company must make "reasonable accommodation for a person's religious needs."
Friends or relatives working for the organization	It is illegal to restrict the employment of a person by reason of the fact that a relative is already employed in the same organization. Some organizations have this question on the application form because they give a financial bonus to anyone who refers a friend or relative for employment and this is the way they track the bonus recipient.
Arrests	It is legal to ask about convictions for a felony within the past seven years but NOT about arrests. The legal rationalization for this is that people of color are arrested far more often than the rest of the population. That being the case, the question of "arrests" becomes discriminatory.
Handicapped	The only person who can assess whether or not the candidate is physically capable of handling demands of the job is a physician. If there are concerns, send the candidate (and therefore all other candidates for the position) for a medical exam. In addition, inform the doctor about the physical demands of the position.
Lowest salary the candidate will accept	It is legal to ask, "What salary are you looking for?" or "How much do you want?" It is NOT legal to ask about the "lowest salary you will accept." This is because women and minorities are willing to accept less compensation than are white males. That being the case, the question becomes discriminatory.

Checking and Giving References and Employer Liability

(See pages 238–244 in the book.) At this time, discuss the issues of checking and giving references, negligent hiring, and employer liability. Ask that participants turn to page 58 in their workbooks and take notes, especially if they check or give references. The main points on which to focus follow:

Reference Checking

Discuss the following points with the group:

- Part of responsible interviewing is reference checking. Generally, this task is handled by the professionals in human resources.

- *If* the hiring manager is expected to check references, he or she should follow these steps:

  1. Ask the candidate to sign a "release" that holds the former employer legally harmless for any information provided.

  2. Do not ask the reference about anything discriminatory or personal such as age, religion, race, national origin, marital status, sexual preference, etc.

  3. Keep the information obtained confidential and on a need-to-know basis.

- Reference checking is a do-it-yourself project; the best ones (most candid and honest) are obtained when the manager for whom the candidate *will* work (*not* human resources) calls the executive for whom the candidate formerly worked. Peers tend to be more open with peers.

- Reference checking should be done by phone or face-to-face.

- Requesting references in writing will produce just the dates of employment and nothing else.

- The least candid reference resource will be the human resource department. They have not had day-to-day contact with the candidate and they are concerned about protecting the company from possible legal problems.

- Asking a person to give a reference is asking a favor. Plan the questions ahead of time and be brief, polite, and considerate of their time. Above all, place the call yourself.

- When references are *not* checked, the organization leaves itself open to a suit for *negligent hiring,* if the hired employee does damage to others in the performance of his or her duties and reference checking would have disclosed this behavior as a pattern from previous jobs.

Reference Giving

Make the point that, because it is fraught with danger, reference giving should be handled by the professionals in human resources. Explain that providing a questionable or negative reference, even if it is truthful, can be grounds for a suit. This is because slander, libel, and defamation of character harms the person from future employment by putting his or her employability in question.

When *giving* a reference, it is legally safe to provide date of hire; date of termination; verification of job title; and verification of salary. Answer the question "Would you rehire?" with one word—either "yes" or "no."

Once again, ask human resources if they have any stories about candidates who were hired without appropriate background checks and who subsequently caused problems that might have been avoided if references had been checked. True stories always make what you are presenting more real to the participants. If you ask human resources to provide some true stories, remember to ask them to disguise the people involved. Further, you should tell the participants that the information is confidential and must not go beyond this room.

Now ask the participants to complete Exercise 9 on pages 59–62 of the Participant Workbook (*Suggested Time:* 15 minutes). Once everyone has finished and checked their answers against the responses given in the workbook, ask the group whether there are any legal issues they wish to go over. Respond to any questions.

PROCEDURE FOR
LIVE ROLE-PLAY ACTIVITY

Time	Materials
One-Day	Transparencies 15–16
1:00—2:00 pm (1 hr)	Participant Workbook, page 63
Two-Day	Overhead projector
9:30—12:15 pm (2nd day)	Colored markers
(2 hr 45 min)	Two flip charts with easels
	Blank transparencies
	Previously prepared role cards

SPECIAL NOTE TO THE FACILITATOR

Because each participant will be using his or her own resume when "playing" candidate, unless your group contains people with similar backgrounds, you will run into the very interesting problem of having a manufacturing manager interviewing an accounting manager for the position of parts and supply supervisor. Should this happen, the person "playing" interviewer will find that the candidate scores virtually zero on all competency areas of the MMM˙. You must not let participants get hung up on this. You might consider matching people with related backgrounds (sales with marketing; accounting with auditing or buying; customer service with sales, etc.) as a way of avoiding this difficulty.

The purpose (the goal or mission) of the role play activity is for the participants to see and experience how their preparation, careful question generation, actual interviewing strategy, and evaluation really work together in a cohesive whole with the MMM® as the central coordinating mechanism. The purpose of the role play activity is NOT to find viable candidates for their vacancies. You may need to remind the participants of this several times during the role-play activity.

Special Materials—The "Candidate Character Role-Play Cards"

In the back of the Facilitator's Guide, you will find thirteen different Candidate Character Role Play Cards on separate sheets. Duplicate them onto colored stock so you can give one or two to each participant at the appropriate time.

These "character cards" serve several very specific purposes. First, they take the sting out of role playing. Secondly, they add a distinctive fun element to the workshop. Third, and most important of all, they provide the answer to the question participants frequently ask, "What kind of interviewing strategy is the best one for me to use?" The answer is that it very much depends on the candidate seated in front of you. For a timid and shy person, using direct questions would be deadly. For a very verbal candidate, direct questions are a very efficient way to redirect the candidate. The only way to make participants realize that their interviewing strategy must be flexible in order to be effective is to ask the role-playing candidates to play various characters. You will want to explain this last point to the participants immediately after the first or second role play when the issue surfaces on its own.

One-Day Format

The following instructions are for the one-day workshop. If you are conducting the two-day workshop, please skip ahead to page 73.

Room Set-Up and Logistics—One-Day Format

Participants should be seated in groups of five at separate tables spaced out throughout the room.

Facilitator's Coaching Activities—One-Day Format

As each group of five role plays, move from group to group, listening in and participating in the feedback process. Here are some of the most common errors you will hear and for which you should provide immediate feedback.

1. Participants beginning all their questioning with "Have you...?" "Would you...?" "Can you ...?" "Are you...?" "Do you...?" These opening words create direct questions. Make certain the participants understand what they are doing and why it is poor technique. Then ask that participants rework the questions so that they become open-ended.

2. Participants asking too many questions at one time (the Barbara Walters technique or the laundry-list question). Here again, interrupt the person. Make sure participants understand what they are doing. Remind them that they should only ask one question at a time. Then request that the person continue the interview.

3. Participants *not* following up on what the candidate has just said. Once again, stop the process. Ask participants to state what they heard when the candidate responded to the last question. Then ask what might be a more appropriate follow-up to the candidate's response. When you catch something of this nature, it is always a good idea to remind the group that, no matter how great their questions are, the follow-up to the candidate's response is where the real treasure lies.

Instructions for the Role Play—One-Day Format

Place Transparency 15 on the projector and refer participants to pages 63 and 64 in the Participant Workbook. Give the group the following instructions:

"I will be moving from group to group as you role play. If your group gets stuck with a difficult problem and you need help, just call me over.

"Each person in each group will have the opportunity to play both interviewer and candidate. Each time a person role plays, it should be with a different person in the group.

"Each interview should take 5 to 6 minutes followed *immediately* by 3 minutes of feedback from the 'observers' or from me if I am seated with your group.

"No matter how interesting, funny, et cetera, the role play might be, please remember that, in order for everyone in your group to have an opportunity to role play, you MUST keep each role play to a maximum of 5 to 6 minutes. Then do feedback. Then have another pair role play.

"Select one person as 'time keeper.' It will be this person's task to alert the group when a role play should end and the feedback process begin.

"When you are playing the *interviewer,* you will need:

1. The MMM® you prepared earlier.
2. A list of prepared questions.
3. A piece of note paper and a pencil.
4. The candidate's resume.

"When you are interviewing, remember to be yourself.

"When you are playing the *candidate,* you will need:

1. Your own resume (it's OK to use one that is out of date) and
2. A 'Candidate Character Role-Play Card,' which I will give you in a few minutes.

"When you are the candidate, remember to speak from your own background, but 'play' the character depicted on your card. Do *not* tell or show anyone your 'role.'

"Anyone not role playing at the moment is to take the part of *observer.* When taking the part of observer, your task is to

1. Pay attention to the interviewer because your feedback should be about interviewing skills.
2. Listen carefully.
3. Take notes on the interviewer's actual words and strategy.
4. Provide feedback to the interviewer when the interview is over about where the person was effective or less effective; particularly good follow-up comments; what the person might have said that would have been a better follow-up; and the interviewer's ability to maintain the observer-catalyst position.

"Here is how we will do the feedback portion:

1. The role players will always comment first.
2. Then the group's observers will give their feedback.
3. Finally, I will comment last if I am at your table.

"Every 'candidate' gets an academy award (*but no feedback on his or her performance*), no matter how the role was played. The idea is to test the ability of the interviewer—*not* the thespian talents of the candidate."

 Place Transparency 16 on the projector, read it aloud, and ask if anyone has any questions. Answer the questions and then begin the role-playing segment.

When the role-play portion has been completed, debrief the activity with the following questions:

- "What have you learned from the role-play experience that you could not have learned any other way?"

- "What was the effect of having the candidates play roles?"

- "What specific unanswered questions do you have as a result of the last exercise?"

The role-play activity should now be complete. It is now 2 p.m. in the one-day session and time for a 15-minute break.

After the break, go back to page 63 in the Facilitator's Guide to lead the next section for the one-day workshop.

Two-Day Format

Room Set-Up and Logistics—Two-Day Format

The workshop is structured to have *two interviews going on simultaneously*: one in front of the video camera in a separate breakout room and one proceeding "live" in the training room with the facilitator.

Thus, you will need someone to assist you by running the video camera. *Make certain this person has a watch* with him or her, because timing is critical. This is what to tell the video camera operator:

> "Please position yourself and the camera so that you can capture *both* role players' body language easily. Each videotaped interview should be 6 minutes long. At the end of 5 minutes, signal the role players that they have only 1 minute of tape time remaining. Let them decide whether to keep going or to conclude the interview. At the end of the sixth minute, simply shut off the video camera and ask the pair to return to the main room. Then get ready for the next pair of role players."

The interviews being taped in the breakout room will be seen by the participants later in the day and critiqued at that time. The partnering assignments, using either method below, are for the pairs being videotaped. For the interviews going on in the main room, ask for volunteers.

Method One: Ask participants to partner with someone who interviews a similar population of candidates (accounting personnel with accountants, IT specialists with IT specialists, customer service managers with customer service representatives, and so forth). This method makes for better learning, but always causes confusion and delay among the participants. It also makes the pairing impossible if the participants come from different areas of the organization.

Method Two: Force the pairing by giving out two sets of numbers as described below. This method is quicker and far less confusing for the participants. However, you may run into the problem of having a manufacturing manager interviewing an accounting manager for the position of parts and supply supervisor. Should this happen, the person "playing" interviewer will find that the candidate scores virtually zero on all competency areas of the MMM®. You must not let participants get hung up on this.

- Suppose there are twenty participants. Make up *two* sets of index cards numbered from 1 through 20, one set in red ink, the other in green ink.

- Tell the group that a *red* number indicates who will play the *interviewer,* while the *green* number indicates who will play the *candidate* role.

- Give out two DIFFERENT numbers to each participant—one red number and one green number.

- An individual's partner in the exercise is the person who has the identical number in the opposite color.

While Pair 1 is being videotaped, ask that Pair 2 *not* volunteer for the live interviews but rather remain "at the ready" to immediately go out to the breakout room as soon as Pair 1 returns. When Pair 2 is being videotaped, ask that Pair 3 not volunteer for a live interview but rather remain "at the ready" so they can immediately go out to the breakout room just as soon as Pair 2 returns, and so on.

You will be controlling the length of the live interviews taking place in the training room. Since you want both sets of interviews to proceed simultaneously, time the live interviews to proceed as follows:

Interview time	5 minutes
Feedback time	3 minutes

(Actually, you will find that feedback is generally accomplished in 2 minutes or less.)

Ask the participants to help you push all the tables together so that everyone is seated in a large circle or square facing one another. Join the group. That way, everyone will be able to hear the live interviews and provide instant feedback to the volunteer role players.

Facilitator's Coaching Activities—Two-Day Format

The group will be looking to you as the expert. Your feedback to the role-playing pair is critical, and the more specific it is, the better. Therefore, write out as much of what you hear as possible. Since the key person in the role play is the interviewer, work on capturing the *exact question asked.* When the candidate responds, attempt to capture the *sense of the response.* Here are some of the critical items you should be listening for and on which you should *be prepared to comment*:

- The structure the interviewer used to begin the exchange;

- Whether or not the candidate answered each question asked;

- If not, whether the interviewer followed up by re-asking the question or if the interviewer failed to recognize that the question was not answered;

- Any "dumb" questions asked by the interviewer;

- Whenever the interviewer failed to follow up appropriately to the candidate's comments;

- How the interviewer made use of direct questions;

- Any use of the tools of silence, clarifying questions, or the parrot technique;

- The amount of conversation carried by the interviewer (ideally about 20 percent) and the candidate (ideally about 80 percent); and

- The interviewer's ability to maintain the observer-catalyst position.

Generally it is better for the learning process if you allow the role play to continue uninterrupted. However, if you hear the interviewer *continually* making some of the most common errors mentioned below, interrupt and provide *immediate* feedback so that he or she can straighten out his or her interviewing technique right away. Here are some of the most common errors you will hear and for which you should provide immediate feedback:

1. Participants beginning all their questioning with "Have you...?" "Would you...?" "Can you...?" "Are you...?" "Do you...?" These opening words create direct questions. Make certain the participants understand what they are doing and why it is poor technique. Then ask that participants rework the questions so that they become open-ended.

2. Participants asking too many questions at one time (the Barbara Walters technique or the laundry-list question). Here again, interrupt the person. Make sure participants understand what they are doing. Remind them that they should only ask one question at a time. Then request that the person continue the interview.

3. Participants *not* following up on what the candidate has just said. Once again, stop the process. Ask participants to state what they heard when the candidate responded to the last question. Then ask what might be a more appropriate follow-up to the candidate's response. When you catch something of this nature, it is always a good idea to remind the group that, no matter how great their questions are, the follow-up to the candidate's response is where the real treasure lies.

Instructions for the Role-Play Activity—Two-Day Format

Give the group the following instructions:

"Each person will have the opportunity to role play four times: twice as the candidate—once live and once in front of the video camera—and twice as the interviewer—once live and once in front of the video.

"The pairings for the video portion will be set up before we begin the actual interviewing process. However, the pairings for the live role plays will be accomplished by volunteering."

Explain whichever pairing method you have selected to the participants and then have them partner accordingly. After you have determined the pairings for the video role plays, make the following points:

"When you are playing the *interviewer*, you will need:

1. The MMM® you prepared earlier.
2. A list of prepared questions.
3. A piece of note paper and a pencil.
4. The candidate's resume.

"When you are interviewing, remember to be yourself.

"When you are playing the *candidate*, you will need:

1. Your own resume (it's OK to use one that is out of date) and
2. A 'Candidate Character Role-Play Card,' which I will give you in a few minutes.

"When you are the candidate, remember to speak from your own background, but 'play' the character depicted on your card. Do *not* tell or show anyone your 'role.'

"Anyone not role playing at the moment is to take the part of *observer*. When taking the part of observer, your task is to

1. Pay attention to the interviewer because your feedback should be about interviewing skills.
2. Listen carefully.
3. Take notes on the interviewer's actual words and strategy.
4. Provide feedback to the interviewer when the interview is over about where the person was effective or less effective; particularly good follow-up comments; what the person might have said that would have been a better follow-up; and the interviewer's ability to maintain the observer-catalyst position.

"Here is how we will do the feedback portion:

1. The role players will always comment first.
2. Then the group's observers will give their feedback.
3. Finally, I will comment last.

"Every 'candidate' gets an academy award (*but no feedback on performance*), no matter how he or she played the role. The idea is to test the ability of the interviewer—*not* the thespian talents of the candidate."

Next, instruct the participants as follows:

"Each videotaped interview will only be 6 minutes long, so do not attempt to squeeze an entire interview into this timeframe. It is not possible. You can begin and end anywhere you like. However, at the end of 5 minutes, the camera operator will signal you that you have 1 minute of tape time remaining. At that point, you can either choose to keep going or conclude the interview. At the end of the sixth minute, however, the operator will shut off the camera and you will be asked to return to the main room."

In the real world, the candidate would know something about the position for which he or she was being interviewed. In the role-play situation this *may not* be true. Therefore, the person playing the interviewer must tell the candidate for what job he or she will be interviewing. However, you do not want the participants to waste a lot of time on this kind of explanation. The focus is to be on the interviewing skills, so in order to stay on point, tell the participants:

"In the role-play situation, it *may* happen that your candidate does not know the position for which he or she is interviewing. Therefore, before starting your interaction, the person playing interviewer should give the person playing candidate a *very brief* 20-second verbal job description before beginning the role play.

"In addition, remember that the purpose—goal or mission—of the role-play activity is for each of you to see and experience how your preparation, careful question generation, actual interviewing strategy, and evaluation really work together in a cohesive whole with the MMM® as the central coordinating mechanism. **The purpose of the role play activity is NOT for you to find a viable candidate for your vacancy.**"

Give each participant two role-play cards, and explain that one should be used when they role play the candidate in the main room and the other should be used when they role play the candidate in the video breakout room.

Direct Pair 1, that is, the person holding the number 1 red (interviewer) card and the person holding the number 1 green (candidate) card to go to the video breakout room.

In the main room, ask for two volunteers to do the first role play. Explain again that they will have 5 minutes to role play, which will be followed by 3 minutes of feedback.

The group will look to you as the expert. It is therefore vitally important that you capture—in writing—as much of the actual interviewing exchange as possible. That way, in your feedback, you can be very specific in quoting the question, the response, and the follow-up.

After 5 minutes of role play, allow 3 minutes for comments and feedback. First comments should be from the role players themselves; second, have the observers make their comments; last, give your feedback.

When Pair 1 returns from the video breakout room, send Pair 2 off and ask for two more volunteers to role play in the main room.

Continue with the process until all participants have had an opportunity to interview in front of the group and on video (both as interviewers and as candidates).

Caution to the Facilitator

Obviously you can see that the timing here is critical. You must keep things moving along at a pretty fast clip in order that all the participants have an opportunity to be videotaped. The video is a fantastic learning tool for both the visual and kinesthetic learners who make up most of your workshop population. Sloppy time management here will cheat some of the participants out of this learning opportunity.

When this activity is complete, it should be about 12:15 p.m. on the second day of the two-day program and time for a 45-minute lunch break.

VIDEO FEEDBACK PROCEDURE (Two-Day Format Only/ Second Day)

Time Materials	Materials
One-Day	Videotape
NA	Video playback unit
Skip to page 81	Overhead projector
Two-Day	Colored markers
1:00—3:00 pm (2nd day) (2 hr)	Two flip charts with easels
	Blank transparencies

For the Second Day Viewing

The second time you will be showing the group a videotape, the tape will be of themselves doing the role plays. Introduce this portion of the workshop by saying:

> "We are now going to see the videotape you all made this morning and discover just how good an instructor I am. Once again, you may find it helpful to take notes, but I'd rather you just concentrate on the tape itself. After each pair, I will stop the tape for a brief feedback session. The feedback rule is that the role players comment first, then any of you can jump in, and finally I will make my comments. Then we will go on to the next pair on the videotape.
>
> "Remember, please, that this is a learning process where we are all trying to help one another get better at interviewing, so do not withhold any negative comments or say complimentary things when a criticism is necessary. No one learns from that—quite the opposite, in fact. So sit back, relax, and here we go."

The video debriefing, from a training point of view, is the most important part of the workshop. You will be seeing just how good an instructor you have been. The debriefing also enables the participants to see, feel, and hear how all the skills, preparation, and strategy come together in a cohesive whole.

Teaching Strategy

Start the videotape. Stop the tape after each vignette. Allow the "actors" to make their comments first. Then ask the group members to comment on what they saw going on in the video in terms of what you have presented regarding interviewing skills and strategy.

You can now add your feedback as well, but only after the participants make their comments. As the facilitator, it is important that, when you give feedback, you tell each "interviewer" what was good about his or her technique. Comment especially on how they began the exchange (using/not using some kind of a structuring statement). It will be helpful if you can take notes during the video so that you can feed back the "interviewer's" exact words, especially when he or she has used a clarifying question, the parrot, a Barbara Walters, or the broken record.

You also want to comment on such things as:

- The interviewer not following up the candidate's responses appropriately.

- The interviewer's overuse of direct questions (answerable with "yes" or "no").

- The interviewer's ability to maintain the observer catalyst position.

Also, let the class comment of the body language aspect, they really seem to enjoy that.

Facilitator Caution: This portion of the workshop can really eat up the time. Keep a watch handy. Do not hesitate to "push" the conversation along so that everyone captured on the video can be seen and debriefed within the alloted time frame.

PEOPLE READING: INTERVIEWING FOR PERSONALITY FIT

Time	Materials
One-Day 3:00—4:00 pm (1 hr) *Two-Day* 3:15—4:15 pm (2nd day) (1 hr)	Transparencies 17–19 Participant Workbook, pages 65–73 Book, pages 180–216 Overhead projector Colored markers Two flip charts with easels Blank transparencies

BEGIN THE SEGMENT by referring the participants to page 65 in the Participant Workbook and by placing Transparency 17 on the projector. Then tell the participants:

> "Up until this point, we have been concentrating on discovering the candidate's skills, background, experience, and ability. [Point to the data shown on the top of the transparency as Step One.] Now we are going to work on analyzing how the candidate is likely to fit into our work environment. This is where we look at the issue of 'personality.' [Point to the word 'personality' under Step One.]
>
> "However, before we can do that, we must take a look at the workplace and analyze what type of personality might work best in the environment into which we will be placing this new employee. [Point to the information at the bottom of the transparency as Step Two.]
>
> "Here we are going to examine the three major characteristics of any workplace environment: the boss, the co-workers, and finally the task responsibilities."

Here are the points you need to make about analyzing the work environment:

Leadership Style

"Let's examine *leadership style* first. It's unrealistic to believe that, as a boss, you can work with anyone. You probably relish working with some people, while others drive you nuts. Since this candidate, if hired, will become a member of your staff, you want to be certain that his or her presence on your team will not create unnecessary stress for you.

"For example, suppose the hiring manager is a perfectionist who expects superior performance from her people. She wants her staff to concentrate on their work and leave any socializing for after-hours. We can assume that she would not want to add a person to her staff who sees work as an opportunity to widen his social circle and use the organization's communication systems for keeping in touch with friends and family.

"On the other hand, if the hiring manager is an outgoing, friendly, social person, we can assume that he would feel some discomfort with a nose-to-the-grindstone type who rarely engages in the minimal courtesy protocols of saying 'Good morning' or exchanging basic pleasantries once in a while.

Nature of Team

"Now let's look at the *nature of the team.* Some work teams require a great deal of interaction; goals cannot be accomplished without the willing participation and active cooperation of every member. Other work teams are really not dependent on one another at all. Each team member has his or her own projects, goals, and customers; the work of one does not impact on the work of another.

"For example, suppose the hiring manager has a staff of congenial and friendly folks who go out of their way to help one another and where projects require the coordination of everyone's individual efforts. That being the case, he would be ill-advised to hire an individual with a 'Lone Ranger,' let-me-work-on-it-by-myself type of mentality. If such a person were added to that group, there would be complaints of non-cooperation, unwillingness to share information, and lack of interpersonal skills. This would harm the overall effectiveness of that manager's department.

Tasks Involved

"The *tasks involved* are also important. Some jobs require a high level of precision and accuracy; there is no margin of error and no tolerance for deviation. Other jobs require a certain amount of adaptability and flexibility.

"For example, if you were hiring a customer service representative, you would probably look for a person who felt comfortable being flexible with rules and who could adapt requirements according to the needs of the customers. On the other hand, if you were hiring a brain surgeon or a quality control manager in a manufacturing setting where the product was pacemakers, you would want a person who was obsessive about accuracy, precision, and doing things right.

Personality Fit

"Once you have a sense of the personality required to fill the vacancy, note that information in the number 1 spot on your MMM® as 'personality fit.' We will be explaining the terms to use in just a few minutes. Using the number 1 spot on the MMM® for this purpose is in recognition of the fact that, even when a candidate possesses all the skills, qualifications, experience, and knowledge required for the position, if the 'fit' is off, the candidate will likely fail in the position."

Background of People Reading

 Now place Transparency 18 on the projector and tell the participants:

"What makes interviewing seem like a great guessing game is that, even when the skills, qualifications, and background are 'right,' the candidate may fail in the new position because of a poor personality fit. Therefore, you need a tool that provides a quick and accurate assessment of the factors that drive the behavior of the candidate.

"The strategy I am going to present requires very little time to learn and almost no effort to apply. Moreover, it provides astoundingly accurate results. It is based on the work of Dr. David McClelland, a professor from Harvard University. It is called *People Reading*.

"Many years ago, Dr. McClelland, in his book, *The Achieving Society*, theorized that a person's relationship to his or her work was based on a sense of self-identity, which incorporates three basic motivational needs: (1) the need to achieve; (2) the need for affiliation, friendship, and acceptance; and (3) the need to feel powerful by assuming a leadership or controlling role over others.

"Every individual possesses some combination of all three motivational drives. When the individual is under stress, however, one of the three—the one that drives most of that person's behavior—will stand out more clearly than the other two.

"An employment interview is a stressful situation for most candidates. That being the case, all the interviewer needs to do is ask a few simple open-ended questions and listen carefully to how the candidate frames his or her responses. [Refer participants to pages 125 and 126 in the Participant Workbook where they will see a list of such questions. You are not going to discuss those questions at the moment, but you do want the participants to know that they are there.]

"Candidates will use specific key words, phrases, or concepts in responding to many different questions. It is as if there is a musical theme playing in the background that they keep repeating. The use of these specific words and phrases over and over is what tells you which motivational need has the strongest influence over the candidate's behavior and personality. Actually, what the candidate is doing is attempting to project to you what he or she thinks is the best kind of person to be—the type that he or she is."

Identifying Candidates' Primary Motivation

 Place Transparency 19 on the projector and leave it on as you go through the explanation of the concept of *People Reading* and how to use it to its best advantage during the interview process.

Utilize two flip charts at this point—one on either side of you. Use the left-hand one to illustrate your points; if you like, draw stick figures, use lines, and create mini-charts. Utilize the right-hand one to record the words and concepts participants are likely to hear from the different candidate types as they respond to questions during the interview process.

To assist you with the delivery of the data in this section, you will find lists of distinguishing information on page 86 of the Facilitator's Guide detailing the various candidate behaviors *during* the interview. This material also appears on page 67 of the Participant Workbook.

Then, on page 87 of the Facilitator's Guide and page 68 of the Participant Workbook is a form detailing the candidate's likely behavior in the workplace *after being hired.* There will not be enough time to discuss the "after hiring information," but you want to be sure the participants know it is there for them to use after the workshop.

Begin by telling the participants:

"People Reading is only about personality fit. It is not useful for determining professional qualifications, experience, probable longevity, skill set, learning ability, or effective management potential.

"Secondly, every candidate is part task-oriented, part affiliation-oriented, and part power-oriented; no one is entirely driven by one single motivation. For the sake of simplicity, however, the candidate descriptions I will be using depict people who are primarily driven by one of the three motivations. I am doing this so that the differences between the three will be thoroughly and completely clear.

"Third and most important of all, *I will put most of the emphasis on those items that are negative.* I do this because, while the good qualities are readily seen in the interview, the negatives are usually hidden. You only discover the problems after the candidate has been hired. I want to show you that you can identify the negatives in the interview and thereby save yourself a ton of problems."

Next, refer participants to page 67 in their Participant Workbooks and review the material on the next page.

Next, again alert participants to the material on page 68 in their workbooks. Tell them that time does not permit you to go through it with them but that it is valuable information they should review on their own.

Note Taking

Explain the following note-taking scheme to the participants (page 66 of the workbook):

"When you interview, write T (task), A (affiliation), and P (power) across the top of your note-taking paper. Each time a candidate says something that indicates a bias toward one of these types, make a mark in the appropriate column. At the end of the interview, you will have some marks in all three columns, but one column will have many more marks than the other two, indicating that this is the candidate's predisposition.

"There are specific word patterns that candidates use in responding to the interviewer's questions that provide the clues as to their central motivational drive.

"For example, the comments made by a task-oriented manager in describing his or her staff ('not very knowledgeable') would be far different from those that would be used by an affiliation-oriented person ('really nice people').

"Since *all* candidates are some combination of task (achievement-oriented), affiliation, and power, you will probably hear a mixture of those identifying words and phrases from everyone you interview. What you want to

Candidate Presentation During the Interview

	Task/Achievement	Affiliation	Power
Words Used	efficient, effective; difficult, challenging; quality, excellence; new, different; dependability, responsibility	nice, cooperation, team effort; needed and helping, happy family; not making waves	uses titles, drops names; wants "more important" work image; caliber; job was beneath me
Body Language	stiff and formal; may fidget; maintains physical distance	nods head "yes"; smiles a lot; maintains close proximity	sits relaxed; spreads out; uses expansive hand gestures
Dress	preference for dark colors	preference for bright colors and patterns	dresses well; well-groomed; may wear initials; may wear or carry status items
Other Behaviors	wants everything in writing; may bring lots of documentation	tells you what he thinks you want to hear; "anxious to please"	asks about org chart, reporting relationships, and promotional opportunities
Demeanor	very serious; minimum of friendly chit-chat; businesslike	relaxed and informal; warm and friendly	manipulative; "salesman" type; slick
References Say	workaholic, compulsive; human relations problems, things are either right or wrong; hard worker	dislikes change; has difficulty making decisions; hard to get a straight answer from; cooperative and pleasant; not a hard worker	works around the rules; quite an ego; likes to impress others; always looking for a deal; too concerned about his/her reputation
Strengths	hard worker; dedicated to excellence and perfection; good problem solver	strong human relations; works without structure	natural leader; good, strong political skills; flexible

Possible Behavior Issues After Hiring

Dimensions of the Work Situation	Affiliation	Power	Task
delegation	haphazard	well-planned	reluctant; partial
concern for quality	reasonable is fine	wants excellence	demands perfection
giving feedback	mostly praises	tells good and bad	mostly critical
temperament	nice guy	even-tempered	moody; angry
about mistakes	accepts as normal	What can we learn?	Whose fault is it?
handling problems	ignores	tries to prevent	likes to solve
organizational skills	disorganized	reasonably organized	precise and exact
making requests	hints	asks and suggests	directs and orders
making decisions	lets fall to others	consults with staff	by themselves
sensitive issues	sympathetic and inquisitive	political and tactful	blunt and tactless
main job interest	acceptance and inclusion	leadership and power	excellence and challenge
self-perception	friend	leader	expert
regard for rules	goes along with	uses and bends	enforces to the letter
biggest problem	decision making	not enough authority	other people
a challenge is	handling change	taking charge	difficult task
human relations	warm and friendly	congenial and objective	cool and distant
work preference	work with others	leadership role	work alone
responsibility	too much already	pushes for more	guards his or her own
staff's ideas	excited but no support	may take credit for	only own are good
handling conflict	runs away	negotiates	confronts

focus on, however, is the quantity of one class of comments over the other two. The determination of the candidate's central motivational drive is made on the basis of quantity. That is why it is important to keep score with your note-taking sheet of paper."

When all these points have been covered and all participant questions have been answered, secure the learning by asking the participants to complete pages 69–70, Exercise 10, in the Participant Workbook (*Suggested Time:* 10 minutes). After everyone has completed the exercise and the scoring, discuss any issues or questions that the exercise generates. Then close this segment by saying:

"In order to create a good 'fit,' it is important to place a task person in a task-oriented job; an affiliate in an affiliate-oriented job; and a power person in a power-oriented job. This is a matter of hiring to strengths. Then the person is comfortable in the job and is not being criticized for who and what he is or for what she lacks.

"More than 90 percent of the candidates who later perform at an unsatisfactory level because of deficient skills, inadequate motivation, poor attitude, or miserable interpersonal skills could have been easily spotted in the interview if the interviewer knew the simple keys to People Reading.

"Untrained interviewers tend to hire in their own image. An affiliate manager will most likely hire an affiliate candidate to join his or her staff; a task-oriented manager will gravitate toward task-oriented candidates when adding to his or her staff; and so on. Hiring in one's own image correlates with the 'halo effect.' It relates to the fact that people are more comfortable around others who think and perceive in a manner similar to how they do. It is only the astute, educated interviewer who can look at the requirements of the position, independent of his or her own personal preferences, and hire according to the specific needs of the job."

WRAP-UP

Time	Materials
Day One	Transparency 20
4:00—4:30 pm (30 min)	Participant Workbook, pages 71–73
Day Two	
4:15—4:45 pm (2nd day) (30 min)	

THE WORKSHOP IS NOW COMPLETE. The participants have been given all the learning the time frame would allow. It is now time for them to test themselves by completing Exercise 11 on pages 71–73 of their workbooks (*Suggested Time:* 15 minutes).

Bring this learning event to a close by placing Transparency 20 on the projector and saying something similar to the following as you sum up the main points of the workshop on a flip chart:

"First, the most important skill in interviewing is listening. You will not learn anything about the candidate if you do all the talking.

"Second, without meticulous preparation, the best person for the job will not be hired. Instead, what you will hire is the candidate who seems most attractive to you at the moment. Candidate attractiveness is dependent on four factors:

- The mood of the interviewer at the time of the interview;
- The number of interviews the interviewer has already been through in trying to fill the position;
- The time of day of the interview; and
- The quality of the previous candidate. (If the previous candidate was a dud, this one will look very good.)

"Third, effective selection requires a sound and dependable recall strategy. Because your interviews will most probably be spread out over several weeks, you need to have a tool that will assist you in clearly remembering the plusses and minuses of everyone you have talked to.

"And last, competent interviewing necessitates separating listening from evaluation. The human mind cannot handle both those tasks simultaneously and do a competent job at both. Usually what suffers is the listening. The MMM® strategy that you have mastered in this workshop will help you separate those two tasks effectively."

REFERENCES

Buckley, M., & Elder, R. (1989, May). The first impression. *Personnel Administrator.*

McClelland, D. (1985). *The achieving society.* New York: The Free Press.

O'Connor, J., & Seymour, J. (1994). *Training with NLP.* New York: HarperCollins.

Resume fraud. (1982, February). *Small Business Report* 8.

Rosenberg (2000). *A manager's guide to hiring the best person for every job.* San Francisco: Jossey-Bass.

Society for Human Resource Management. (1990, December). *Personnel Journal,* pp. 58–61.

CANDIDATE CHARACTER ROLE-PLAY CARDS

FEARFUL and CAUTIOUS

You have been looking for work for two years. Your family has suffered greatly during that time, and you do not wish to repeat that experience. If this position is offered to you, you will accept in a minute. What worries you is being put into a job where you have to make decisions or respond to anything controversial. The last time you stuck your neck out and did something creative, you found yourself out of a job.

The key to being job safe is to keep your head down and your mouth shut. Any suggestion you might have, any decision you might make, could conflict with management's ideas. You cannot risk jeopardizing another job and your family's future. If asked, you will always be the voice of caution, asking how things have been done before. In this interview, you will use cliches so as to avoid saying anything controversial.

Instructions for Playing Your Role

1. Do NOT look at each other's roles.

2. Please play your role conscientiously.

3. Do not overact; be natural.

4. Emphasize the behavior described above.

UNINVOLVED and UNCOMMITTED

You have heard that working at this company is a pretty good deal. The benefits are good, and the pay is very attractive. You've also heard that the management likes its people to work hard. You are a master at looking busy. Your last manager actually thought you were a regular nose-to-the-grindstone type. You have developed a no-nonsense exterior that keeps most people at a distance and protects you from becoming too involved with what's going on. You do just enough to get by. You take on as few assignments as possible, especially those that might result in overtime. You work so you can afford to spend time on activities outside of work such as sports events, theater, sailing, skiing, and travel.

Today the important buzz words in landing a job are "excellence," "service," and "quality." Your previous work experience has taught you that lip service to those concepts is all that's required. No one really cares about those things; it's just window-dressing for the customers.

Instructions for Playing Your Role

1. Do NOT look at each other's roles.

2. Please play your role conscientiously.

3. Do not overact; be natural.

4. Emphasize the behavior described above.

AGGRESSIVE and ARGUMENTATIVE

Another interview! You can hardly wait. If there's one thing you can't stand it's having to explain why you've had so many jobs. People just refuse to appreciate how extremely valuable you are. Every company has hired you because of your knowledge and expertise and then let you go because of your inability to get along with others. "Not a team player," they told you.

Your solution is: Don't put me with idiots and wishy-washy people who say they don't know how to do something or have no opinion on how something should be done. If managers would just get rid of their incompetent people, you wouldn't be so critical and judgmental of your co-workers. It isn't your fault that these supposedly capable people are so stupid.

Instructions for Playing Your Role

1. Do NOT look at each other's roles.

2. Please play your role conscientiously.

3. Do not overact; be natural.

4. Emphasize the behavior described above.

THE FAST-TRACKER

You have had a superior education from one of the nation's premier universities. Your first job was with an old-line company that "sold" you on its goal of striving to be at the forefront of its industry. They said they wanted new blood with fresh ideas—creative dynamos who were not afraid to take risks. During the two years you have been with that organization, you have found that any new idea has been systematically killed by management that feels threatened by change. Although rapidly losing market share because of its out-dated technology, the company was unwilling to invest any more in research. Any financial resources were poured into expanding their sales efforts.

If you remain with that organization, you will either become technically obsolete or unemployed. You need to find a new job as quickly as possible, one that will challenge you and give you the opportunity to work with high caliber people with state-of-the-art technology.

Instructions for Playing Your Role

1. Do NOT look at each other's roles.

2. Please play your role conscientiously.

3. Do not overact; be natural.

4. Emphasize the behavior described above.

THE RELUCTANT CANDIDATE

You have a long commute and a job, which you love, that often stretches well beyond the boundaries of an eight-hour work day. You're beat by the time you get home and often feel overwhelmed by the arguments that ensue as soon as you walk through the door. Your older child will be fighting with the younger one about who is supposed to do the dishes and both will fight with you when you mention homework. Your spouse will start an angry discussion asking you to find another, less demanding job. You are starting to dread coming home.

To please your spouse, you have decided to look for a new employment situation, one where you will have very minimal overtime and a commute no longer than 20 minutes. You fully expect that, whatever the new job will be, you probably will NOT enjoy it. This thought makes you miserable, but you have decided to make the sacrifice in order to save your marriage.

Instructions for Playing Your Role

1. Do NOT look at each other's roles.

2. Please play your role conscientiously.

3. Do not overact; be natural.

4. Emphasize the behavior described above.

THE LONE RANGER

You have been working with an organization that has gone from sensible top-down management to the flaky format of teams. Not only is group composition always changing, but the company's priorities are in flux as well. In the beginning, you had your own projects and your priorities were always clear. Now it's just total confusion.

You positively HATE working in groups. There is always more talk than action; more interpersonal friction than necessary; and more controversy over priorities and work methods than required. Worst of all, if the team is successful because it utilized your idea, you have to share the glory with the others. You want to be an individual contributor again—where you work by yourself and take responsibility for both your successes and your failures. You are tired of battling over every little thing and then having to share the results of your creativity with others who are not as innovative or experienced as you are.

Instructions for Playing Your Role

1. Do NOT look at each other's roles.

2. Please play your role conscientiously.

3. Do not overact; be natural.

4. Emphasize the behavior described above.

NEGATIVE MENTAL ATTITUDE

You have been totally frustrated in your miserable job for two years. Decisions are a struggle requiring approval from seven levels of management, most of whom have no idea what your requests are all about. Most of your day is spent in pointless meetings. The CFO has a strangle-hold on company funds. Human resources does not allow poor performers to be fired without endless amounts of paperwork. Your staff are unmotivated but very clever; they know how to appear busy but they actually produce few results. Your boss excels at schmoosing but refuses to deal with problems. You were promised promotional opportunities and salary increases, neither of which has occurred. You want a work situation where people are motivated, management is not bureaucratic, promotional opportunities are plentiful, and salary increases are sizeable and regular. You want to feel that your time is not being wasted by people who are just there for a paycheck.

Instructions for Playing Your Role

1. Do NOT look at each other's roles.

2. Please play your role conscientiously.

3. Do not overact; be natural.

4. Emphasize the behavior described above.

IN THE BAG

You are under no pressure to impress anyone. You are currently employed in a job that you like; the work is challenging, the boss is nice, and the pay is good. So at this point, you feel very relaxed about your candidacy for this particular position.

You feel you already have the job (in the bag) if you want it and that the interview process is merely a formality. You were referred to this company through a head hunter who has assured you that you are the perfect candidate for this position. After seeing your paperwork, the company indicated that it was very interested in making an immediate job offer.

You are anticipating that the interview will be more of a pleasant chat where the two of you will try to get to know one another a little better. Naturally, during the interview you will try to learn more about the organization and this particular job opening.

Instructions for Playing Your Role

1. Do NOT look at each other's roles.

2. Please play your role conscientiously.

3. Do not overact; be natural.

4. Emphasize the behavior described above.

ANXIOUS TO PLEASE

From experience, you have learned that the best way to impress interviewers favorably is to be pleasant and agree with everything they say. So, in this interview, you intend to do a lot of smiling and to respond affirmatively to as many questions as possible.

You will certainly not say anything negative about yourself or your experience, even if asked. Should the interviewer mention some troublesome or difficult topic and you are unable to figure out where he or she stands on the issue, you will attempt to evade the issue altogether by insisting that, whatever the situation is, it will not be a problem.

You will let the interviewer know—tactfully of course—that you like him or her and that you are impressed with the difficulty of the interviewing task as well as the person's fine interviewing skills.

Instructions for Playing Your Role

1. Do NOT look at each other's roles.

2. Please play your role conscientiously.

3. Do not overact; be natural.

4. Emphasize the behavior described above.

TIMID and SHY

Interviews are difficult for you because you are basically a very shy person. In any work or sales situation, you are generally very well-prepared for any questions that might come up. This is because you are quite knowledgeable about what you do. Interviewing, however, is a different animal entirely. Here the interviewer has the expert knowledge, whereas you know very little. Moreover, the interviewer is sitting in judgment of you, your skills, your career choices, and your very existence.

Knowing you are being judged means that making eye contact is virtually impossible for you. You have found that, by looking at the floor or out the window, your discomfort eases a bit. Often, because you are nervous, your voice cracks. That being the case, you will try to speak as little as possible and let your rather impressive resume speak for you.

Instructions for Playing Your Role

1. Do NOT look at each other's roles.

2. Please play your role conscientiously.

3. Do not overact; be natural.

4. Emphasize the behavior described above.

THE TURNABOUT

You are very serious about finding another position in this industry. To that end, you have been interviewing with many of the firms involved in this type of business. You know that your particular skills are in demand, so there is no doubt that any of these firms would really like to have you aboard. You want to be certain, however, that you have all the facts about every opportunity out there so you can select the best employment situation for yourself.

There are five points you want to make regarding your skills and experience. Beyond that, you intend to satisfy your curiosity regarding all aspects of the job opening (current projects, number of people in the department, number of people on the various teams, how much latitude there is regarding decision making and risk taking, promotional opportunities, how often performance is reviewed, the size of a typical merit raise, how often raises are scheduled, etc.). That means you will be seizing the initiative in the interview and asking many questions of the interviewer.

Instructions for Playing Your Role

1. Do NOT look at each other's roles.

2. Please play your role conscientiously.

3. Do not overact; be natural.

4. Emphasize the behavior described above.

THE KNOW-IT-ALL

There is no one who knows more about this kind of work than you do. Not only have you had years of varied experience in this field, but you have also worked in many allied areas as well. You have a Ph.D. and several post-doctoral certificates. In addition, you have trained others in the field in both work and university settings. Often you are asked to make presentations at conferences and meetings about new developments in the field.

This company would have to be really stupid not to offer you a job. But then, interviewers are not the brightest people in the world. You will therefore have to make your superior expertise blatantly clear to this interviewer. You may even have to tell him or her that it would be ridiculous to even consider anyone else.

Instructions for Playing Your Role

1. Do NOT look at each other's roles.

2. Please play your role conscientiously.

3. Do not overact; be natural.

4. Emphasize the behavior described above.

POLITICALLY CONNECTED

You know a lot of important people in the community. For one thing, you are a close friend of the local state senator, with whom you often play golf. Moreover, your next-door neighbor is the executive vice president of the company. In fact, it was he who suggested you drop by to see if there were any openings that might suit your background and interest.

You have taken the time to read the job openings posted in the human resources department and realize that you do not possess all of the qualifications listed. However, considering who recommended that you apply, that should be no problem. You will just have to let the interviewer know about your powerful connections. You are certain that having influential friends in high places will go a long way in getting you into this company and into a well-paying job.

Instructions for Playing Your Role

1. Do NOT look at each other's roles.

2. Please play your role conscientiously.

3. Do not overact; be natural.

4. Emphasize the behavior described above.

TRANSPARENCY MASTERS

Transparency 1   THE COST OF TURNOVER

Basis: yearly salary of $45,000/year for the new employee	
Inadequacy of the new employee (1 year)	$20,800
Assistance to new employee by co-workers	14,350
Decline of productivity before departing	2,600
Attention of staff on departing employee	900
Position vacant or with stop-gap fixes	21,750
HR processing of both employees	1,085
Recruitment (ads, agency fees, etc.)	2,890
Orientation by operating department	2,930
Relocation	0
TOTAL COST	$67,305
RATIO OF COSTS TO AVERAGE SALARY	1.55%

Source: *Personnel Journal*, December 1990.

1. Personal Preferences of the Interviewer

2. Personality Traits of the Candidate

3. Educational Background of the Candidate

4. Behavioral Skills of the Candidate

Hiring the Best Person for Every Job by DeAnne Rosenberg. Copyright © 2002 by John Wiley & Sons, Inc. Published by Jossey-Bass/Pfeiffer.

TRADITIONAL

Tasks

Activities

Responsibilities

NEW FORMAT: JOB OBJECTIVES

Results

Output and Deliverables

Achievements

Your Performance Expectations

Transparency 4 PERFORMANCE EXPECTATIONS WORKSHEET

What expectations, when fulfilled, will I regard as satisfactory performance?

Position Title: _____

The key responsibilities for this position are	The performance level that I will consider satisfactory is	This is how I will measure performance:	Based on my expectations and the performance I expect, the candidate will need these competencies:

Hiring the Best Person for Every Job by DeAnne Rosenberg. Copyright © 2002 by John Wiley & Sons, Inc. Published by Jossey-Bass/Pfeiffer.

Transparency 5 MASTER MATCH MATRIX®

POSITION: _____

Needs ——→   ——→ Wants

Candidate's Name:	first priority competency	second priority competency	third priority competency	fourth priority competency	fifth priority competency	sixth priority competency	seventh priority competency	eighth priority competency	Total score:

Hiring the Best Person for Every Job by DeAnne Rosenberg. Copyright © 2002 by John Wiley & Sons, Inc. Published by Jossey-Bass/Pfeiffer.

Transparency 6 COMPLETED MASTER MATCH MATRIX®

POSITION: Administrative Manager

Needs ⟶ ⟶ Wants

Candidate's Name:	Two years' experience supervising	Delegation & coaching skills	Participative leadership style	Conflict management skills	Goal setting as a management strategy	Superior communication skills	College graduate	Professional appearance	Total score:
Agnes Jones	8	3	2	1	0	1	0	0	15
Phil Aline	7.5	5	6	5	2	2	1	1	29.5
Joseph Potter	8	6	6	5	2	1	2	1	31
Hannah Spolling	8	3	5	5	2	3	1	0	27
Louise Baker	4	7	6	3	2	3	2	1	28
Connie DeLessie	7.5	7	6	5	4	3	2	0	34.5
Oscar Lemoninen	4	7	3	2	0	1	2	1	20

Hiring the Best Person for Every Job by DeAnne Rosenberg. Copyright © 2002 by John Wiley & Sons, Inc. Published by Jossey-Bass/Pfeiffer.

Transparency 7 MASTER MATCH MATRIX®

POSITION: _____ your assistant

Needs ➝   ➝ Wants

Candidate's Name:	first priority competency	second priority competency	third priority competency	fourth priority competency	fifth priority competency	sixth priority competency	seventh priority competency	eighth priority competency	Total score:

Hiring the Best Person for Every Job by DeAnne Rosenberg. Copyright © 2002 by John Wiley & Sons, Inc. Published by Jossey-Bass/Pfeiffer.

STRUCTURING THE 40-MINUTE INTERVIEW

COURTESY INTERVIEW

First 20 minutes of the interview

Use for best area of information gathering

Make "go/no go" decision

SELL THE JOB

Second 10 minutes

Answer candidate's questions

SECOND BEST AREA OF INFORMATION GATHERING

5 minutes

THIRD BEST AREA OF INFORMATION GATHERING

5 minutes

Transparency 9 BODY LANGUAGE AND TRUTHFULNESS

1. Interviewer asks a question

2. Interviewer observes candidate's physical reaction (immediate body language response)

3. Candidate responds verbally

   If body language and verbal response match—probably truthful

   If body language and verbal response do NOT match, truthfulness is questionable

4. If there is a discrepancy, the interviewer should ask a clarifying question

Hiring the Best Person for Every Job by DeAnne Rosenberg. Copyright © 2002 by John Wiley & Sons, Inc. Published by Jossey-Bass/Pfeiffer.

How Important Is Body Language?

How We Communicate

7% of the message is conveyed by words

38% of the message is conveyed through voice

55% of the message is conveyed through body language

Source: R. Birdwhistell. (1970). *Kinesics and context: Essays on body motion communication.* Philadelphia, PA: University of Pennsylvania Press.

Hiring the Best Person for Every Job by DeAnne Rosenberg. Copyright © 2002 by John Wiley & Sons, Inc. Published by Jossey-Bass/Pfeiffer.

Transparency 11   USING SILENCE EFFECTIVELY

Working Assumption:

Candidate Has Two Mental Lists "At the Ready,"

One of Positives (A) and One of Negatives (B)

Interviewer Asks a Self-Appraisal Question

Interviewer Waits Through 20 Seconds of Silence

Candidate Responds with Positive (A) List Data

Interviewer Waits Through 5 Seconds of Silence

Candidate Responds with Negative (B) List Data

Hiring the Best Person for Every Job by DeAnne Rosenberg. Copyright © 2002 by John Wiley & Sons, Inc. Published by Jossey-Bass/Pfeiffer.

Transparency 12   QUESTIONS USED IN INTERVIEWING

1. Direct Questions

2. Open-Ended Questions

   Puzzle Questions

   Behavioral Questions

3. Clarifying Questions

4. Self-Appraisal Questions

Transparency 13   WHAT IS A "DUMB" QUESTION?

1. Telegraphs the Desired Response

2. Offers a False Choice of Responses

3. Answers Are Obvious but Cannot Be Checked for Truthfulness

4. Question That Just Fills the Silence and Allows the Interviewer Thinking Time

Hiring the Best Person for Every Job by DeAnne Rosenberg. Copyright © 2002 by John Wiley & Sons, Inc. Published by Jossey-Bass/Pfeiffer.

1. Employing the interviewer's words to make up a related question and then answering the manufactured question

2. Asking the interviewer a laundry-list question as a clarifying question

3. When given a choice of responses (laundry-list question), the candidate asserts that both alternatives are accurate

4. Using some plausible excuse in declining to respond to the question

Transparency 15   ROLE-PLAY GUIDELINES

OBSERVERS

Listen

Take Notes

Give Feedback

INTERVIEWER

Be Yourself

Use Matrix and Questions You Prepared

See Candidate's Resume

CANDIDATES

Use Role Cards

Use Your History

Have Fun

TIME

5 minutes for interviews

3 minutes for feedback

QUESTIONING STRATEGY FOR ROLE-PLAY ACTIVITIES

FOR CANDIDATES

Any closed-ended questions should be answered "YES" or "NO"

FOR INTERVIEWERS

Every question should begin with "WHAT," "WHEN," " WHERE," "WHO," "HOW," or "WHY" (use "why" sparingly)

FOR OBSERVERS

Any "Barbara Walters" questions should be corrected immediately

Give feedback on opening, follow-ups, and observer-catalyst stance

EFFECTIVE PLACEMENT

STEP ONE: Evaluate the Candidate

Qualifications

Skill, Experience, Knowledge, Ability

Personality

STEP TWO: Evaluate the Vacancy

Leadership Style of the Manager

Nature of the Work Team in Place

Requirements of the Tasks Involved

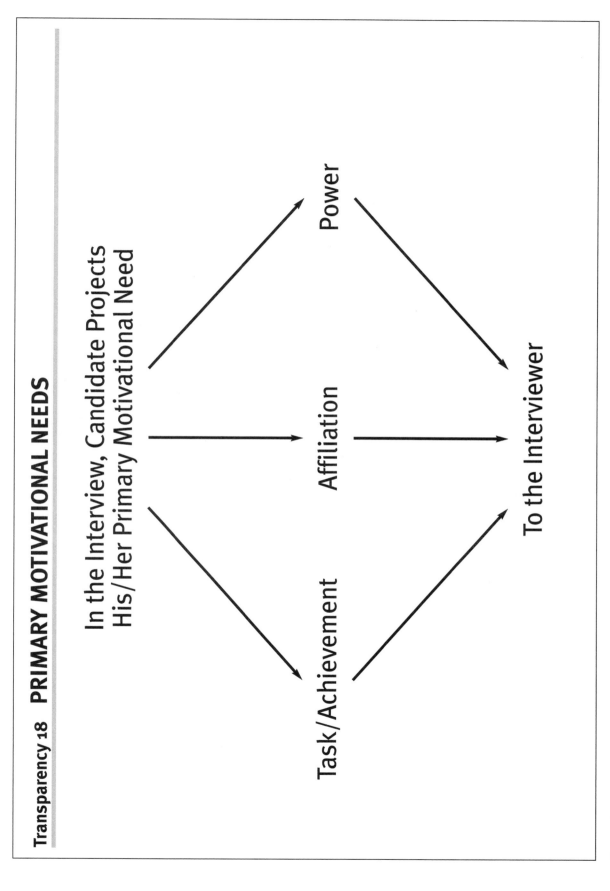

Transparency 18 **PRIMARY MOTIVATIONAL NEEDS**

In the Interview, Candidate Projects His/Her Primary Motivational Need

Power

Affiliation

Task/Achievement

To the Interviewer

Hiring the Best Person for Every Job by DeAnne Rosenberg. Copyright © 2002 by John Wiley & Sons, Inc. Published by Jossey-Bass/Pfeiffer.

PEOPLE READING AND PERSONALITY FIT

Candidate Portrayal During the Interview

Candidate Representation	Task/Achievement	Affiliation	Power
Demeanor	businesslike, formal	warm, social	manipulative
Speaks About	goals, responsibilities	co-workers	status, titles
Your Impression	competitive	cooperative	egocentric
Best Competency	hard worker	human relations	leadership
Work Preference	by him- or herself	group member	leader role
Human Relations	low priority	most valued quality	opportunity for manipulation/influence
Self-Perception	expert	friend	leader
Communication	earnest, honest	personal, social	political, strategic

Hiring the Best Person for Every Job by DeAnne Rosenberg. Copyright © 2002 by John Wiley & Sons, Inc. Published by Jossey-Bass/Pfeiffer.

Transparency 20   MAJOR CONCEPTS

1. The most important skill in interviewing is listening

2. Without meticulous preparation, the best person for the job will not be hired

3. Effective selection requires a sound and dependable recall strategy

4. Competent interviewing necessitates separating listening from evaluation

Hiring the Best Person for Every Job by DeAnne Rosenberg. Copyright © 2002 by John Wiley & Sons, Inc. Published by Jossey-Bass/Pfeiffer.

ABOUT
THE AUTHOR

DeANNE ROSENBERG has been speaking professionally at business meetings and conventions for over twenty-five years in both the United States and Europe. She was the first woman to speak under the auspices of the American Management Association.

She has taught via satellite in the United States and has presented multiday courses on management in the United States, Great Britain, Canada, South Africa, Mexico, and Italy (in simultaneous translation). She has written numerous magazine articles that have appeared in the business press both in the United States and abroad. In addition, she has authored several film scripts focusing on motivation and performance improvement, some self-study programs for AMACOM, and several cassette programs on communication skills. Her book on interviewing, *A Manager's Guide to Hiring the Best Person for Every Job,* was published by John Wiley & Sons in 2000.

Ms. Rosenberg's articles have been published in *Industry Week, Quality Digest, Executive Excellence, Supervisory Management, International Journal of Manpower* (Great Britain), *Association Management Magazine, Successful Salesmanship* (South Africa), *Business Credit, Aftermarket Today, Quality Observer, Continuous Journey, Real Estate Professional, Executive Development* (Great Britain), *Industrial Distribution, NonProfit World, Human Resource Management, Journal of Healthcare Materiel Management,* and *Managing Technology Today.*

Her corporate clients include IBM, United Airlines, Digital Equipment Corporation, Fidelity Investments, Harvard Medical School, Dole Fresh Vegetables, Sebastian International, Biogen, Anheuser-Busch, Boston College, NYNEX Information Systems, Stratus Computer, Genrad, Dentsply International, McDonald's, General Motors, and Rockwell International. Her government and military clients include the U.S. Department of Commerce, the Social Security Administration, the General Services Administration, the U.S. Army Finance and Accounting Center, U.S. Naval Undersea Surveillance, the U.S. Army War College, the Internal Revenue Service, Defense Logistics, Soldier Systems Command, Camp Pendleton, U.S. Department of Defense, U.S. Postal Service, and Wright Patterson Air Force Base. Her association clients include The Associated General Contractors, *INC* magazine, American Hospital Association, Federally Employed Women, National Business Forms Association, American Society of Association Executives, and Toastmasters International.

Ms. Rosenberg is a Fellow of the Workforce Stability Institute and a member of the National Advisory Board of the President's *Strategies and News Magazine*. She holds memberships in the American Society for Training and Development and the National Speakers Association, which awarded her the coveted Certified Speaking Professional (CSP) designation in 1985. She is a graduate of Bryn Mawr College and is listed in the *World Who's Who of Women.*

She can be reached at deanne@deannerosenberg.com.

HOW TO USE THE CD-ROM

System Requirements

Windows PC

* 486 or Pentium processor-based personal computer
* Microsoft Windows 95 or Windows NT 3.51 or later
* Minimum RAM: 8 MB for Windows 95 and NT
* Available space on hard disk: 8 MB Windows 95 and NT
* 2X speed CD-ROM drive or faster

Netscape 3.0 or higher browser or MS Internet Explorer 3.0 or higher

Macintosh

* Macintosh with a 68020 or higher processor or Power Macintosh
* Apple OS version 7.0 or later
* Minimum RAM: 12 MB for Macintosh
* Available space on hard disk: 6MB Macintosh
* 2X speed CD-ROM drive or faster

Netscape 3.0 or higher browser or MS Internet Explorer 3.0 or higher

NOTE: This CD requires Netscape 3.0 or MS Internet Explorer 3.0 or higher. You can download these products using the links on the CD-ROM Help Page.

Getting Started

Insert the CD-ROM into your drive. The CD-ROM will usually launch automatically. If it does not, click on the CD-ROM drive on your computer to launch. You will see an opening page. You can click on this page or wait for it to fade to the Copyright Page. After you click to agree to the terms of the Copyright Page, the Home Page will appear.

Moving Around

Use the buttons at the left of each screen or the underlined text at the bottom of each screen to move among the menu pages. To view a document listed on one of the menu pages, simply click on the name of the document. To quit a document at any time, click the box at the upper right-hand corner of the screen.

Use the scrollbar at the right of the screen to scroll up and down each page.

To quit the CD-ROM, you can click the Quit option at the bottom of each menu page, hit Control-Q, or click the box at the upper right-hand corner of the screen.

To Download Documents

Open the document you wish to download. Under the File pulldown menu, choose Save As. Save the document onto your hard drive with a different name. It is important to use a different name, otherwise the document may remain a read-only file.

You can also click on your CD drive in Windows Explorer and select a document to copy it to your hard drive and rename it.

In Case of Trouble

If you experience difficulty using the *Hiring the Best Person for Every Job* CD-ROM, please follow these steps:

1. Make sure your hardware and systems configurations conform to the systems requirements noted under "Systems Requirements" above.

2. Review the installation procedure for your type of hardware and operating system. It is possible to reinstall the software if necessary.

3. You may call Jossey-Bass/Pfeiffer Customer Service at (800) 956-7739 between the hours of 8 A.M. and 5 P.M. Pacific Time, and ask for Technical Support. It is also possible to contact Technical Support by e-mail at *techsupport@JosseyBass.com.*

Please have the following information available:

* Type of computer and operating system

* Version of Windows or Mac OS being used

* Any error messages displayed

* Complete description of the problem.

(It is best if you are sitting at your computer when making the call.)